Flight of the Sparrow

Flight of the Sparrow

A Collection of Inspirational Adventure Stories

Earl Nance

12/3/2013

Rev. Earl Nance

LIFE SENTENCE
——Publishing, LLC——

www.lifesentencepublishing.com

Like us on Facebook

Flight of the Sparrow – Rev. Earl Nance

Copyright © 2013

Scripture quotations are taken from the Holy Bible, King James Version, Cambridge, 1769.

PRINTED IN THE UNITED STATES OF AMERICA

First edition published 2013

LIFE SENTENCE Publishing books are available at discounted prices for ministries and other outreach. Find out more by contacting info@lifesentencepublishing.com

LIFE SENTENCE Publishing and its logo are trademarks of

LIFE SENTENCE Publishing, LLC
P.O. BOX 652
Abbotsford, WI 54405

Paperback ISBN: 978-0-9832016-4-9

Ebook ISBN: 978-1-62245-086-2

10 9 8 7 6 5 4 3 2 1

This book is available from www.lifesentencepublishing.com, www.amazon.com, Barnes & Noble, and your local Christian bookstore

Cover Designer: Jeremiah Zeiset

Editor: Mary Vesperman

Share this book on Facebook

Dedication

This book of true short stories is lovingly dedicated to Rebecca, my wife of forty-four years, and our three children, James, Angela, and Mike, as well as their seven children.

The purpose in my writing these stories is to show the richness and joy of being part of a God-fearing family, and the excitement of living an excellent adventure with the Lord leading the way and His providing for our every need in His time.

Perhaps others will be encouraged to step away from the ordinary and be encouraged to live an excellent life of adventure in serving the Lord with their whole heart and life. This will only occur by moving in the direction of the Lord, being active in His work wherever we are, and doing those things that He makes available. We are only limited by those restrictions that we place on the relationship. The only people whom the Lord will use are those who make themselves available, and as we move in His direction, He begins to give us opportunities and challenges.

Joy comes from reflecting on just what the Lord is accomplishing while He allows us to be tools for His work, as we witness the victories He lets us be a part of. Seeing the Spirit of the Lord work in the lives of others is a wonderful thing. Our joy as believers and followers of Jesus is not based on our circumstances; it is based on our relationship with the Lord.

I pray that YOU will be encouraged to experience this joy that comes from serving the Lord with YOUR life.

Love in Christ,

Earl Nance, Missionary Evangelist

Contents

CHAPTER 1

Torment of a Soul

I t was a hot and humid evening, with very little air stirring on the last night of the evangelistic gospel tent meeting. The man, in his seventies, was sitting with his wife in the back row of chairs, quite obviously not enjoying himself any more than he had the night before, but it was encouraging to see him there.

The message that evening was about trying to hide behind a hypocrite while God is calling you. It is a very uncomfortable place to hide, because both the hypocrite and the person hiding are pretending to be something that they are not. Our personal relationship with God does not depend on what someone else is or is not doing; it only depends on what we are doing with our own life and testimony. How can we possibly think that another person's wrongdoing will be bad enough to serve as a screen we can hide behind, while we ourselves are not obeying God? I believe that this is often tried, but never with any measure of success.

I try to never identify a potential problem without offering the remedy, which is to admit our wrong to God and turn from it by beginning to do what is right. God knows us and what we are doing, but loves us anyway, enough that He sent His Son Jesus to offer His own blood in payment for our wrongdoing. What is required of us is to humbly accept that payment and His forgiving love. As Lord of our life, Jesus will change it and make of us what He wants us to be. His plan for our life will be much more rewarding than anything we ever could have done.

Upon inviting people to make decisions for Jesus, either to accept Him as their hope of heaven, or to re-dedicate their life to Him, this man lifted his hand asking me to pray that he could come to the understanding that he would belong to Jesus and be able to spend eternity with Him in heaven. After praying for him and others, and leading all who would consent to pray aloud in prayer, asking Jesus to forgive and save them, they were asked to make their decision public by coming forward and telling a personal worker about the decision they had made. This is based on what we read in the Bible: *Whosoever therefore shall confess me before men, him will I confess also before my Father which is in heaven. But whosoever shall deny me before men, him will I also deny before my Father which is in heaven* (Matthew 10:32–33).

No one else responded to the invitation, and when it was over, we dismissed in prayer. Everyone started leaving the tent except this man and his wife. He sat back down with his head in his hands, weeping aloud. His lips were moving as though he was earnestly talking to someone. Seeing his anguish of soul, I went over and sat in the chair beside him and asked if he would like to talk. He shook his head, indicating that he did not want to. Not wanting to leave him in this condition, I placed my hand on his shoulder and gently told him that Jesus loved him, and so did I. We just sat there quietly for a short time and he began to talk between sobs. He began by saying that he did not want to go to hell but did not know how to avoid it; he didn't think that Jesus could ever love him. We quietly and patiently took the Bible and together discussed the following several verses: *For God so loved the world, that he gave his only begotten Son, that whosoever believeth in him should not perish, but have everlasting life. For God sent not His Son into the world to condemn the world; but that the world through him might be saved. He that believeth on him is not condemned: but he that believeth not is condemned already, because he hath not believed in the name of the only begotten Son of God* (John 3:16–18).

We then went to John 10:28–30: *And I give unto them eternal life; and they shall never perish, neither shall any man pluck them out of my hand. My Father, which gave them me, is greater than all; and no man is able to pluck them out of my Father's hand. I and my Father are one;*

And we then finished with a reassuring promise from Romans: *That if thou shalt confess with thy mouth the Lord Jesus, and shalt believe in thine heart that God hath raised him from the dead, thou shalt be saved. For with the heart man believeth unto righteousness; and with the mouth confession is made unto salvation. For the scripture saith, Whosoever believeth on him shall not be ashamed. For there is no difference between the Jew and the Greek: for the same Lord over all is rich unto all that call upon him. For whosoever shall call upon the name of the Lord shall be saved* (Romans 10:9–13).

As we got near the end of these verses, his countenance began to change. He seemed more at peace and began telling me of a few tragic events that had occurred in his family, but he made it clear that he did not blame God, nor was he mad at God. It was amazing that this should come out now that he had made peace with God. When we have peace with God, His peace alters our lives, and our whole outlook often changes completely, always for the better.

After this, we went to the food area, ate, and he then pitched in helping to take down the tent and load the chairs and equipment. As we parted that evening, it was a joy to see the love of Jesus begin showing in his life, as he was able to lay his heavy burden down at the feet of Jesus. I pray that I will never tire of seeing Jesus change lives.

CHAPTER 2

Safe on a Rainy Night

The week had been long and was getting longer. I had spoken in St. Louis on Monday; Galesburg, Illinois, on Tuesday; Trenton, Missouri, on Wednesday; and back to Chicago, Illinois, where I spoke twice on Thursday and four times on Friday. Then I was to drive to Greenwood, Indiana, to pick up over fifteen hundred New Testament Bibles and Gospel of John and Romans booklets that were provided to *Sparrow Ministry* by Bearing Precious Seed, a ministry of Berea Baptist Church in Greenwood, for distribution. After speaking nine times, witnessing fifty-six people ask Jesus to be Savior and Lord of their life, and driving many miles, I still had one project to finish the work week: going the 465 miles, or about eight hours, that would take me home.

Before leaving Greenwood and seeing those Golden Arches, I decided that it would be a great place to dine on their Southern Style Crispy Chicken sandwich, a favorite of the *fluffy sparrow*, even though, I must confess, it seems rather foul – perhaps even cannibalistic –for one bird to be eating parts of another. After my meal, I left in the rain for home. As you can imagine, after driving a while in the warm, comfortable car with the rhythm of the windshield wipers and the constant rain, and my appetite satisfied, it was getting about nap time. By now I was about halfway across Illinois, so I decided to park and rest for a while. I carry with me a long, comfortable, down-filled black coat with a hood, so if I am in the wet or cold, I can wrap up and be safe from the elements. This night it was both wet and cold. I slept for about an hour, and then took off again toward home, passing over the Mississippi River into Missouri, even though it was raining harder by now. While driving, I usually set the cruise control to avoid going either too slow or too fast (the *fluffy sparrow* seems to have a heavy foot), but on a very wet road, the standing water kicks it off, and it had done so a number of times. I was really beginning to feel tired again while pressing forward, just wishing that I was already home, but I still had at least two hours to go, which would have me home around two o'clock Saturday morning. Putting a Southern Gospel CD in the player and turning it up loud, and turning down the heat to get a little fresh air, I settled in to finish the project. About then, I drove through quite a bit of water, which I thought had turned the cruise control off, but it would not reset. Pressing the gas would not make it go either. Then I discovered the source of the problem: Not only was *I* about out of gas, but the *car* was actually out of gas too.

Having made that mistake before, I carry with me a one-gallon container of gas, so if it were to happen again, it wouldn't be that big of a problem. So I coasted to a place where I could get off the road and not get stuck. With all but a minimum number of lights on, I got out in the rain, being glad that I already had my *fowl* weather gear on. I took the gas container and eventually was able to get some of the gas in the car, even though I knew I had spilled some. There went the possibility of going between twenty to twenty-five miles before having to get more.

The car started after some cranking, and I began driving. Then I checked with my know-it-all GPS, who goes by Gertrude, or Gerty for short, and she gave me the addresses of many gas stations, most of which were out of my limited range, but there were three that were less than seven miles ahead. That was great news, so I went to the first one, discovering it was no longer a gas station. The next one was closed, perhaps for good, having no lights on at all. The last chance was Casey's, and while lights were on at the pumps and some night lighting on in the store, all else was dark because they were closed. By now it was after midnight. I could not leave without gas, so I just decided to park it there, in front of the pump. Letting the back of the seat down some, I zipped the coat up, pulled the hood down over my face, leaned back, and went soundly to sleep.

Several hours later: What was that noise? It sounded like a phone. It was my cell phone. Who could be calling at that time of night was the question that came flooding into my cocoon. Uncovering my head while grabbing the phone, I noticed all the lights were on at the station, and another car was fueling on the other side of the pump. Rebecca, with urgency in her voice asked, "Where are you?" At first, being half awake, I kinda wondered how she had found me, but she had, so I told her where I was, what had happened, and that I would be home after a while. I was glad that she had called, knowing the station had been open for at least ten minutes. Getting out of the car, I expected to be stiff and sore. I was quite surprised that I wasn't and proceeded to fuel the car.

It seemed to me that I should go in and explain why I had spent at least part of the night there. I was surprised that there was seemingly no alarm in the face of the person I told this to, like it was every day that you came in to open the station and there is a big body wrapped in black, reclining in a car with its head covered, and it wasn't moving!

Now I had gas, coffee, and rest, so it was time to go on home. I started the car, pulled out of the drive, and the CD player began playing this song:

His arms are holding holding, His spirit surrounds me.

Every step I take here below, I am never alone.

In my trials there's sweet peace, as onward I go.

My hand is in the hand that shall never forsake me,

And I know I'm in the center of His will,

So whatever storm be-tide. He will still be there to guide,

As I'm safe in the arms of Jesus

Now my feet, though they get weary, oh they will never falter,

And my eyes, though they be blind, they can clearly see, clearly see,

The strong hand of Christ my Savior, leading onward!

I'm His and He belongs to me.

My hand is in the hand that shall never forsake me,

And I know I'm in the center of His will,

So whatever storm be-tide, He will still be there to guide,

As I'm safe in the arms of Jesus

– Author Unknown

What a blessed thing the Lord did that night, allowing me to run out of gas and go to a place of comfort and safety, knowing that I needed rest and was not smart enough to stop and get it. All the while, He lovingly supplied all my needs. There is nothing in this life that is as satisfying as serving the Lord. Thank You, Jesus!

CHAPTER 3

Attempting to Win a Devil Worshiper to Jesus

I was informed at a rescue mission recently that there was an avowed devil worshiper in attendance. The man that was pointed out to me was one who had walked past me earlier. I had noticed that he avoided eye contact, which in itself is not unusual, but with that, he seemed to project that I was not welcome in his presence. He had many markings of the world of rebellion, including many ink markings on his arms and some on his face and neck. All other skin was covered with black clothing. At least it covered the rest of his tattoos. His hair was dark and slicked back, and in his mustache I noticed a couple of black beads that were suspended by a wire loop that went through a piercing in his nose (quite similar to a hog ring in a pig's nose or a ring in an unruly bull's nose). One thing was for sure: he had not come to hear me speak about Jesus' love for him. The leader that evening asked me to try to address this man's condition and to reach him with truth.

Not knowing how to do this without isolating his lost condition and leaving everyone else believing that they were not that bad, the Spirit of God led me to speak of all false religions, which all result in the same destination: ETERNAL TORMENT IN HELL with the devil and his angels. Knowing that I did not have the courage or wisdom to do this on my own, I assured myself, *Ye are of God, little children, and have overcome them: because greater is he that is in you, than he that is in the world* (1 John 4:4). I just opened my mouth, and in the strength of the Lord, let the words pour out. I, and the people there that night, named and discussed several false religions. We started with Islam, included Buddhism and the cults who all use the Bible along with their own phony prophets' writings, and ended up with those who worship the devil, pointing out their common lack of hope in the life to come. I even asked them, if their religion was so good, why were they not at their homeless shelter instead of this Christian one?

After practically alienating almost everyone, I began to preach Christ and Him crucified. I told them of the love that God the Father and Jesus His Son demonstrated in offering payment for our sins, forgiving us if we repent, and giving us eternal life with the Father and Son in heaven, and companionship while still here on earth. We began to see the Spirit of God do His work in the hearts of these men. Upon circling the landing spot several times, the *fluffy sparrow* finally came in for a touchdown. WOW! While giving the invitation for people to receive Jesus as Savior, many men prayed the sinner's prayer aloud with me, asking Jesus to be the Lord of their life and promising to follow and obey Him as Master and Lord. I asked those who had really done business with God, and were serious, to stand up in testimony of their decision to follow Jesus. There were around twenty who stood up, and after asking those who had rededicated their lives to the Lord to also stand, there were a total of thirty-three men standing out of the sixty who were in attendance. We rejoiced in the victories, but were saddened that the target, the devil worshiper, left that evening seemingly just as bound by the devil as he had been when he came in. It is my hope that he will have another chance to become free from the bondage of sin and death.

What I learned from this story is that the Lord honors willingness and faithfulness. We may not achieve our goals, but the Lord always honors the effort and will use it to His pleasure.

CHAPTER 4

First Tent Meeting Set-up

The big day had finally arrived when all of our dreams, talk, plans, and collection of parts and supplies for conducting a gospel tent meeting was to become reality. Just a few days before the great yet traumatic event of setting it up, Pastor Denny stood in the pulpit, looked me in the eye and said, "The only reason that we have for not serving the Lord is that we are either afraid or lazy." I would hate to admit either one of those conditions, but admittedly, it is much easier to plan to do something out of the ordinary than to actually do it. Some call it procrastination, but Denny correctly calls it what it is.

Deacon Wayne Boley of Freedom Baptist Church in Brookfield, Missouri, and I had been on a scouting trip around small towns in the Brookfield area to find a place to hold our tent meeting, and we decided on several possible locations, which included the Rothville city park. We contacted a few people around town, including the city clerk, and made arrangements to set up in their park May 20–22, 2010.

The townspeople appeared to welcome us, because the day after we had arranged it, they had a tree that had fallen down completely removed and cleaned up, the grass mowed and trimmed nicely, and the outhouse fixed (maybe that's because they heard we would be serving ham and beans.) Now I was without excuse or reason to delay any longer.

We advertised the meeting in the local shopper, which has a large circulation, scurried around trying to get all the parts together, and tried to imagine all the little things that could go wrong, and the things that we may need to put it all together, including preparing and serving food after each meeting. All seemed to be coming together. Having never done this before, nor ever having the privilege of speaking with anyone who had, we were entering uncharted waters. Speaking of water, I began looking at the long-range weather forecast, which was calling for rain on all three days of our meeting. This couldn't be. It wasn't in our plans! It would be too muddy to park! People wouldn't come out in a cold rain to sit in a tent for preaching, even though there would be hot ham and beans and Rebecca's best homemade cornbread. (You will have to ask her for the secret old family recipe.) Well, not to worry, the forecast would just have to be wrong. Well guess what? It wasn't wrong. On the Thursday morning I was to meet Wayne to set up the tent, it was pouring rain and had been for a couple of days. I called him about the time we had expected to start, and we agreed to meet for lunch at an eating establishment in Brookfield to discuss what we would do.

Our discussion began by our agreeing that we did not want to do this in the rain. (My granddaughter Emily once told me, as I was giving her a reason why we were not doing something I had agreed to do, "Grand Pa, everyone has one." I said, "Has one what?" She replied, "An excuse!") BUT Wayne and I decided that even though we would get wet and people probably would not come, we would go ahead and do what we said we would do. Perhaps this was just a test from God to see whether we were serious or not. Doesn't the Bible tell us: *for He maketh his sun to rise on the evil and on the good, and sendeth rain on the just and on the unjust* (Matthew 5:45b)? While asking the blessing on the food that we were about to eat, I told God that we were going to do what we said we would do, whether it rained or not, even though I would really appreciate it if, in His permissive will, He would cause it to stop raining until after our meeting was over.

We decided that we needed more help, so Wayne was going to try to get a couple of people to help us get it done, while I would go on out to the park and begin putting the tent together. I walked out of the eating establishment, hoping it would not be raining, but it still was and continued to do so. Upon arriving at the park, I got out in the rain, put on my raincoat, and began sorting out tent parts. This tent was made of two 20-foot-by-20-foot tents, connected together to make one big tent. It had a pipe frame without any center post, and seemed to be a regular giant set of tinker toys. (I loved Tinker Toys as a child, which probably partially prepared me for this experience.) Wayne returned, along with our help, and by then it was just sprinkling a little. We put the top cover on, and then lifted it up, putting the legs under it. By now it had stopped raining completely. We then put the second one up in a fraction of the time, fastening the two of them together and tying the whole thing down. Before having everything completely together, people began to show up. Wow! *If you build it, they will come* was more than just a slogan from a worldly movie.

Twenty-two people were there that first evening, as we sang some songs, had special music, did a few seemingly magic illusions as a promised attraction for children of all ages, and then spoke on who Jesus is and was and that He is coming again, from Revelation 1:1–19. At the end of the service, we had plenty of ham and beans, having planned on about one-third of a pound of each and half a pan of cornbread per person. Needless to say, after it was all said and done, we had enough food for another go at it.

When the meeting was over and everyone had gone home and everything was put up, I got in my car and was starting to back out of the park's driveway because it was too muddy to turn around in, and it began pouring down rain. Would you believe that? Some may say that it was just chance, but I believe that God, in His mercy and grace, heard my prayer, and knowing my heart, showed me a little bit of His favor. You may believe whatever you will, but I believe in the loving power of God.

The ground was soggy the second night, and each time I sat in a chair, it seemed like my legs were getting longer, or was that the chair heading for China taking the most direct route? The third night the weather was beautiful, and during the invitation, there were at least two people who made important decisions for Jesus.

Two men at the eating establishment told us that we were crazy for going out to set up a tent in the rain. I told them that I had let the devil make a fool of me for the first thirty years of my life, so now I guess it would be no problem being crazy for the Lord Jesus, doing whatever I possibly could to tell others of Jesus' love, mercy, grace, and salvation.

> Trust in the LORD with all thine heart; and lean not unto thine own understanding. In all thy ways acknowledge him, and he shall direct thy paths (Proverbs 3:5–6).

CHAPTER 5

Demonic Invitation Interruption

I t seemed as though there was a restless spirit of despair and hope-lessness in the crowded, warm, musty-smelling room. There were over two hundred men setting in rows of chairs, some watching *Perry Mason*, others trying to sleep, with others playing games or just talking. Security personnel came in and turned off the giant-screen television while I was setting up my sound system. It looked like it was really going to be a challenge to get even minimal atten-tion from these men who likely would rather have been somewhere else, but they had nowhere to go, and probably didn't have a way to get there if they did.

I started the Bible study by trying to lead them in the first verse of *Jesus Loves Me,* being as cheerful as I could possibly be. There was little response the first time, so we tried it two more times. A few more people joined in, probably thinking that I would never shut up if they didn't start singing a little. For the most part, it is a different group of men each month, but there are some who have been there for several months, day after day of the same thing. Sometimes they have enough people who do want to sing, and they really do it well.

It is a thrilling thing to see grown men who have very little to smile about, start moving their lips and singing about the love of Jesus for them. Often they begin to smile a little, and it is as though I can see the lights in their eyes come on. This was not one of those days.

Remembering why I was there, I began telling them of their worth to Jesus – how they were created in His image and likeness, but because of sin, the Spirit of God needed to be reborn in their lives. Jesus had made it all possible by shedding His innocent blood for them on the cross of Calvary, dying for their sins, and rising from the dead on the third day. After many people witnessed His resurrected state, He then ascended into heaven with the promise that He would return for those who would believe in Him and call on Jesus to forgive them, asking Him to be the Lord of their lives. There was much more to the message than this simple framework. It seemed that some were listening, judging from the response to the three main questions I always ask, and having them lift their hand if their answer is yes. The questions were: (1) Are you sure you would go to heaven if Jesus came back today, or if you were to die today? Do you have evidence of that because He has begun changing your life since you came to know Him? (2) Of those who know Jesus, are there any who would want me to remember them in prayer, because they would be embarrassed if they were to stand before Jesus today? They need help to get victory over those troubling things in their lives? (3) Are there those here today who are not sure of their relationship with Jesus, and would like for me to pray for them so they could be confident they belonged to Jesus and will be with Him when He comes or if they die before He comes? With that, I began praying for the saved, and for those who had problems, and then I encouraged those who wanted to know Jesus as their hope of heaven to believe that Jesus did rise from the dead, and to confess that belief with their mouth, as I led them in prayer, asking them to pray aloud with me.

We had just begun to pray the sinner's prayer together, with several people praying with me aloud, when there came quite a commotion bursting into the room. I stopped praying to see what was going on, and there was one man, probably in his early thirties, kind of leaping along, waving his arms and hands, and cursing very loudly, taking the name of the Lord in vain, and using every profane word I had ever heard, along with many vulgarities. By now he was near the back of the room and started moving across the back. It looked as though he would come up the other aisle, then cross back across the room, coming directly within my reach. I was silently asking the Lord, *What should I do? Confront him in the name of Jesus? Or run for my life?* Having never been much of a runner, I began to imagine what I might say, and what his response probably would be. I had to remind myself: *Ye are of God, little children, and have overcome them: because greater is he that is in you, than he that is in the world* (1 John 4:4). About then, he turned and started out the way that he had come in, never quieting or settling down. By then a security man had come in and met him and was rewarded by the man cursing him. In his wisdom, the security man did not touch the madman but rather began moving toward the door to the hallway, leading him out of the building. As I heard the man being escorted out of the building, I called the people in the room to attention again by telling them that the devil did not like what we were doing and had done his best to stop it. But the devil lost this round, and I also called their attention to the fact that they had just witnessed about the best the devil had to offer them if they didn't come to Jesus, who is a good and loving Master. With that, we began with the sinner's prayer again. This time there were more people praying, and they were praying with more intensity. When I asked those to stand in testimony to their having asked Jesus to be their Lord and Savior, there were thirteen who stood. Truly we can sing, *Victory In Jesus* and believe that it is so.

> *Delight thyself also in the LORD: and he shall give thee the*
> *desires of thine heart. Commit thy way unto the LORD; trust*
> *also in him; and he shall bring it to pass* (Psalms 37:4–5).

The desire of my heart is to be used by the Lord as a messenger of His mercy and saving grace.

He grows sweeter each day as I follow Him and see His mighty hand at work.

CHAPTER 6

Searching for More

The *Sparrow Ministry* has been blessed over the years in seeing many souls make positive decisions for Jesus, with each new year bearing more fruit than the year before. That is the kind of progress I have always wanted to see. I hope to never be satisfied merely remembering victories of yesteryear. With this mindset, I, the *fluffy sparrow*, began looking for additional places to go fishing for men.

There are a few truisms about fishing: (1) there are often more fish in bigger ponds; (2) fish never come to you, so you must go to them; (3) the more frequently one fishes has a lot to do with how many fish one catches; and (4) one must like to catch fish or they probably will not go fishing for very long. With these facts in mind, and hearing about *all that thar gold way out there in Cal-i-for-ni-a,* and seeing the opportunity at last to go and check it out, I got in the *sparrowmobile* to go have a little look-see. I was disappointed at what I found.

Rebecca and I began the twelve-day journey by stopping in Omaha, Nebraska, where I was already on the calendar to speak. The next afternoon we stopped in Denver, Colorado, at the Denver Rescue Mission, arranging to go back and speak November 30. I have heard that they have some stunningly beautiful weather around that time, and we do seem to enjoy a challenge. Two days later, we stopped in at the rescue mission in Las Vegas, Nevada. The program that evening included hip-hop music, or very loud noise, along with the message being presented in the form of rap noise, magnifying droopy drawers and street-gang clothing, along with the crooked ball cap, even during prayer. It was no surprise to see that no one wanted to accept Jesus as their Savior that evening. We returned the next morning for their "church service," and while it was a little more tolerable, it met with the same results. I had no desire to go back. It was not the big pond that it had been made out to be. I spent that Lord's Day evening at the only rescue mission I could find that had an evening chapel service. It was not mandatory for their guests, so as expected, there were more people outside of the service than there were inside. They were constantly walking in and out disrupting the service, and there seemed to be no one to do anything about it. The speaker that evening was Fred Soles, who did an excellent job of presenting salvation through Jesus alone and the need that everyone has of Jesus. There were some decisions made, both on the men's and women's sides. That demonstrated the power of the Holy Spirit being able to work, even in the middle of mass confusion. Again, this was a much smaller pond than I had expected it to be. If everyone there had been seated, it would have been fewer than three hundred people. The next day I drove to San Diego to see what the situation was there, and it held less promise for the *Sparrow Ministry* than anything we witnessed west of Denver. I had planned originally to return to Las Vegas, and then go to Salt Lake City, Utah, but I began to see the bigger picture.

Have you ever seen a cow standing knee-deep in lush green grass with its neck stuck through the fence, straining to get a mouthful of some old weed? I have, and reflecting on the ministry the Lord has already given me and what I thought I wanted to do, it put a bad taste in my mouth, along with a knot in my stomach, causing me to decide that I wouldn't be able to get home quickly enough. Instead of visiting a few more places, it became perfectly clear to me that the Lord had designed this trip for me so I could appreciate so much more the ministry He has led me to.

Since returning to the Midwest in the last three weeks, we have been blessed in seeing over 240 souls accept Jesus as their Lord and Savior or re-commit their lives to Jesus. I have heard it said, "Look to see where the Lord is working and go there." Silly me. I am already there, and unless the Lord calls me somewhere else, here is where I intend to spend most of my time. My very nature has always led me to want to expand whatever it was that I was doing, but perhaps I should relax and enjoy doing what the Lord has given me to do without pressing the fences.

If the Lord wants me in another pasture, He will open the gate and drive me out of the old one.

I pray that I will fully submit myself to the will of the Lord and be totally led by Him.

> Perhaps I will be better off understanding and accepting this portion of Scripture: *Trust in the LORD with all thine heart; and lean not unto thine own understanding. In all thy ways acknowledge him, and he shall direct thy paths* (Proverbs 3:5–6).

CHAPTER 7

St. Paul, Minnesota, to Chicago, Illinois, One Snowy Day

One winter morning in January of 2010, after spending the night in the hotel at Union Gospel Mission in St. Paul, Minnesota, I had the challenge of driving the four-hundred-mile trip to Chicago, Illinois. There had been quite a bit of snow and other wintery weather traveling from Trenton, Missouri, the day before, with a forecast of much more to come across the path where I was scheduled to go.

Of course I was tempted to call in sick, because it is next to nauseating to think of heading out into a winter storm, but when your calling is to tell homeless people of the loving mercy and grace that Jesus has afforded to hopelessly lost sinners, you just prayerfully get in the car and go where you have agreed to go. It is not that there is no one else who can do it, but the opportunity to serve as the messenger of the Lord had been given to me that day, and how could I expect each day to be a sunny one?

That evening in St. Paul had been well worth the drive, having the privilege of witnessing twenty-eight men make decisions for Christ, some accepting Jesus as their Lord and Savior, and others rededicating their lives to Him.

It had continued to snow and blow through the night and wasn't expected to stop for some time, so I did the only sensible thing left to do: I got in the car, started the engine, had a short prayer meeting, set the GPS for Chicago, put it in gear, and went on my way. The GPS is a poor substitute for my wife traveling with me, but it has a female (I think) voice, gives me lots of directions, and will really visit with me if I make a wrong turn.

As I traveled out of St. Paul, it was very slow-going for the first ten miles, with the traffic coming into town at a near standstill. The howling wind caused a subzero windchill. I was thankful that the heater in the *sparrowmobile* worked great, and that I had enough fuel to drive about an hour before needing to refill. I left before breakfast and was looking for those familiar Golden Arches, anticipating having a wonderful dollar-menu sausage biscuit with some strawberry preserves to help it go down, and settle in. I was beginning to wonder if I had made a terrible mistake, as I hadn't come upon the Golden Arches yet, and feared that the car and I would both run out of fuel. I believe the car could have handled it better than I could have. Finally, a bit farther down the road, I spotted them: the Golden Arches. Things seemed okay again.

After getting filled up, and regaining courage, I got in the car and started out again. I hadn't gone very far when I saw the first pickup truck in the median with its wheels pointed to the sky. Within about ten miles, there were at least three more pickups, and several SUVs, all on their tops. The more I saw, the tighter I held the steering wheel, and the slower I went. The really remarkable and quite noticeable thing was that whenever a big gust of wind would come and the car would begin to slide, it was as if there was a force greater than the wind that would straighten everything out and calm me down. Do you think that the eye of the Lord might have been on the *fluffy sparrow*? I certainly believe it was.

This verse brings real meaning to me in times like this: *For he shall give his angels charge over thee, to keep thee in all thy ways. They shall bear thee up in their hands, lest thou dash thy foot against a stone* (Psalm 91:11–12).

CHAPTER 8

God Mends Broken Things for His Use

I was on the way home from Tulsa, Oklahoma, on July 27, 2010, and was rushing along, in a hurry to get home, because I had already been away two nights. This night would be a short one, because I was scheduled to speak in Omaha, Nebraska, the next evening, 571 miles from Tulsa by way of Trenton.

Some unusual things began happening to the *sparrowmobile*. Lights began to periodically get brighter, then dimmer. After a while the cruise control quit working, and then after about another half-hour, the speedometer went back to zero. Luckily I was still paying attention and did not get out of the car at that time. I was still going seventy miles per hour according to the GPS. Later the turn signals were not working as they should, and the radio and CD player began changing stations on its own. Frankly, in the dark of the night on a long, lonely road, it was kind of freaky, kinda like entering the Bermuda triangle, never to return. As you might expect, I did make it home. The next morning I checked the voltage output of the alternator, which was too high, so I took it to a mechanic, hoping to have it repaired that morning. They checked it and confirmed what I had already found, but they couldn't fix it then, so off I went to another shop, where I was told that if it had that problem, my car would probably have a lot more than that wrong with it, and would possibly cost more to repair than the car was worth.

Rebecca and I were planning to take this car to California on a mission survey trip for me, and a business trip for her, in about three weeks. This was the only "reliable" transportation we had, and now what were we going to do?

In despair and desperation, I went home and had a talk with Jesus. I admitted that this was beyond my means, out of my control, and I had no idea what to do about it. Would He please help me? As I was chattering away in prayer, it was as if I clearly heard the words in my mind, *Earl! Be quiet and wait upon the Lord.* Wow! You mean that I could just be quiet and You would solve the problem, Lord? Upon admitting that the problem was out of my control, and asking the Lord to meet the need in His time, I waited. Three hours passed and it was about the time that I should leave for Omaha, Nebraska. There were no phone calls, no new car keys in the mailbox, or any other thing like that, but I couldn't just sit there and wait. I would take my older van, the one with 365,000 miles on it, loaded with over 1,500 pounds of women's clothing to take to Chicago. The air was not working, but at least it would probably get me to Omaha. When I left home to get the old van at my shop, which is across town, I decided to go by the auto parts store to get a repair manual, so I could learn how to fix the *sparrowmobile* later myself.

When I got back in the car to go to the shop to get the other van to leave for Omaha, the strangest thing happened. The speedometer was working fine, so I tried the cruise, and it also worked as it should. With these essentials working, would it be too much to ask for the radio and CD player to also work? I tried them and they also worked, as well as the turn signals. I could hardly believe my eyes! Then the old devil began impressing me with doubts, making me wonder if it really would make it, or would I just get out of town and be stranded hundreds of miles from home?

I determined in my heart that if the Lord fixed it, it was fixed, and how could I doubt Him when I had just asked Him to help me? I would not want to insult the Lord with my doubts, so taking the *sparrowmobile* to Omaha was the only sensible thing I could do. Of course, the devil was not done trying to discourage me. Such thoughts as, *This is not faith; it is foolishness. Earl, you don't really think that God fixed your car, do you? How absurd! You have had broken cars before, and God didn't fix them. Why would He do it now? Do you really think that God is always going to keep your car running?* Truly, no, I do not, but it is running now and I needed it.

If I had listened to all the devil's reasoning, I would never have experienced the joy of victory the Lord prepared for me. Since then, I have driven that car over six thousand miles, and even though I have replaced the radio, the essentials have caused no problem whatsoever, and I do not expect them to. I must admit that as I've witnessed the Lord do so many unusual things, I have come to expect the unexplainable. The Lord is teaching me to trust Him with all my heart, not leaning to my own understanding, and in all my ways acknowledge Him, and He will direct my paths (see Proverbs 3:5–6).

Contrast

While traveling on Highway 400 from Wichita, Kansas, to Tulsa, Oklahoma, one warm, dark night, I was on my monthly circuit ride to bring the message of hope in Jesus to homeless people. I was weary from the heat of the long day and was trying to stay cool by spending time walking around in cool stores and drinking senior coffee at the Golden Arches. (Wonder why they never check to see if I am old enough.) I was waiting for evening to tell some of the homeless in Wichita about the Jesus who loves them and will save them when they accept what He did for them on Calvary's cross. I had spoken to a group of men at the Salina [Kansas] Rescue Mission the night before, witnessing several men make various decisions for Jesus and many rejecting Him, and had spent that night in my hot mini-camper. (When tired enough, I can sleep almost anywhere, as some preachers I have sat under could tell you. It was not their message; it was my lack of ability to stay awake. Promise!) This night, on my way to Tulsa, I decided to pull over and rest, lest I carelessly enter the "eternal rest" through a life-ending crash. (Will Rogers once said that when he died, he wanted to do like his granddad did – just drift off to sleep, never to awake, not like the rest of the people in the car who were screaming in terror. I do not share his desire.)

I stopped to spend the night in my mini-camper, the Pontiac Montana van, at one of the most scenic rest stops on that highway. Believe it or not, it is an acceptable accommodation, especially compared to what is used by those the Lord has led me to minister to. If one likes a warm room, stay at a rest stop in the summer; or, if one prefers it cooler, do so in the winter. There are many wonders of life that can be discovered while traveling this way. One of these discoveries while in such cramped quarters is the joy of bathing with a "handy wipe." I have discovered that no matter how cold it gets, those wonderful towelettes do not freeze. They are still soft and pliable at fifteen degrees. I must admit that it takes almost more courage than I have to take a sponge bath with a handy wipe at that temperature, because it is just too refreshing. That was not going to be one of my problems on this morning.

Morning had come, and what a gloriously beautiful day it was. It was cooler now, around seventy-five degrees, with a nice breeze blowing. The sky was a lovely shade of blue with a few puffy white clouds slowly traveling along, and from this hilltop, I could see the expanse of rolling hills that were covered with nature's carpet of green with a few splashes of red, yellow, and violet color provided by God's wildflowers.

Coming around the drive as I left the rest area to return to the highway, I was startled by the contrast that I saw. On my right side was the beautiful scenery that I have attempted to describe, including the tall grass swaying gently in the breeze like the gentle waves on the ocean, and a few small herds of cattle scattered in the meadows, while on my left side was a busy highway with cars and trucks climbing fast in both directions to go over the crest of the big hill, along with the constant noise of engines and tires. And just beyond that was a wind farm of at least a hundred windmills churning away, attempting to make green energy. They sure do not improve the green scenery.

I stopped the car to write this story from this location, and what I am looking at can be compared to the contrast in my life with and without Jesus. I was trying to find satisfaction in life with the clamor, noise, pleasures, and business of the world, which left me empty, while on the other hand, the peace and refreshingly sustaining love of God was available all the time. All that was required of me to receive it was to turn my eyes and heart toward Jesus, accepting Him as my Lord and Savior.

This was one of those divine appointment moments, because from a CD that was in the player from the day before, with over twenty songs on it, "Turn Your Eyes Upon Jesus" began to play, which caused me to come to these stated conclusions. Here are those refreshing words:

Turn Your Eyes Upon Jesus

O soul, are you weary and troubled? No light in the darkness you see?

There's light for a look at the Savior, and life more abundant and free!

Through death into life everlasting He passed, and we follow Him there;

O'er us sin no more hath dominion – for more than conqu'rors we are!

His Word shall not fail you – He promised; Believe Him, and all will be well:

Then go to a world that is dying, His perfect salvation to tell!

Turn your eyes upon Jesus, look full in His wonderful face,

And the things of earth will grow strangely dim,

In the light of His glory and grace.

– Helen Howarth Lemmel

CHAPTER 10

Somewhat-Willing Reluctant Witness

For some time, I had been talking about wanting to try street preaching, but I had talked to so many people for so long that I had begun to convince myself that it seemed all I wanted to do was talk about it, and it would probably never happen. Still wanting to talk about it, I was having lunch with a friend and once again mentioned my alleged desire. He asked me the unthinkable, "Earl, when and where are you going to do this?" (Thanks, Jesse, maybe you were just tired of listening to me ramble about something that I was probably never going to do, or the Holy Spirit used you to challenge me.)

Whatever the reason, my response was, "Next week when I go to St. Louis to speak at the mission, I'll go a few hours early. Weather permitting and if it is not against the law, and if I can find a place to do it, being able to get the attention of a few people, I may try it."

The day had arrived to begin this adventure in evangelism, and I was about to be on my somewhat reluctant way. First, I must check the weather in St. Louis. Often, it is much more severe there than it is here in Trenton, and one must be careful in planning. I turned on the computer and searched the Internet, trying to find some reason not to do this today. Much to my dismay, everything was going to be good to go. At one point on the way, I began to relax, as there were a few clouds in the sky, suggesting the possibility of a good, solid reason to postpone this project to a more convenient time, but they soon passed. I was left without excuse. Driving on to downtown St. Louis, I found a big park in front of the old capitol building that was framed by the big arch on the Mississippi River. This was a place that many people frequented; it would be where I would try this thing.

There was a man sitting on a park bench with a few bags, appearing to possibly have no place to go. Seeing parking meters, I parked my car and, without show, began praying mostly for myself. "God, don't you think this grass out here needs a little water? How's about a little un-announced pop shower, or better yet, a big rain storm?" God did not answer those prayers, but He did send a policeman on a bicycle who stopped to talk to the man on the bench. I sat there appraising the situation and realized that this could be the window of opportunity I had hoped for.

Picking up my Bible with my left hand and a bunch of gospel tracts in my right, I got out of the car, walked up to the policeman, and somewhat rudely interrupted him. Speaking louder than usual, while holding my Bible and kinda shakin' it, letting it fall open like I was fixin' to start reading, I asked him, "Is it okay to preach the gospel of Jesus Christ on the streets of St. Louis?" (I guess I was thinking that if I acted crazy like David did before he became acting king of Israel, when he was taken before a king who was at war with Israel, that this policeman might tell me to get back in my car and leave, which would have completed my mission.) It did not work; instead, he looked me right in the eye with a serious but kind look, and what he had to say I am not sure I was willing to hear.

He said, "Not a problem," causing me to ask, "Do you mean to tell me that it is okay for me to just start preaching right here on this sidewalk?"

He said, "Sure, but if there begins to be a crowd, and they begin to block the street, we would need to move them off the street." (I'm thinking, *Is this guy serious, or just funnin' me?*)

I then asked him, "Do I need some kind of permit [still searching for an excuse]?"

He kindly said, "No, you don't need a permit; you can preach anywhere you want to in St. Louis."

What was I to do? Here I was in downtown St. Louis, on a beautiful afternoon, my Bible in one hand and some gospel tracts in the other, and people in the park. While unsuccessfully trying to be asked to leave but wanting to retain a little spark of credibility, I decided to pass out some tracts. At least I wouldn't have to say too much, and if someone asked, I would be there to tell them how to get to heaven from St. Louis, Missouri.

There was a group of men sitting on some benches about half a block away, so I walked over to give them some tracts. Perhaps they would need something to read while they were having their beer break. While walking by, giving each man a tract, one said to me, "Our dad was a preacher." He said that one of the other men was his twin brother. I asked him if his dad ever did any street preaching, and he told me, "Not that I ever knew of." Then asking him how often he came to this park, he told me that it was almost every day, and had been doing so for several years. I then inquired whether he had ever seen anyone do any preaching in the park, and he told me that he had not. This was really NOT building my confidence. I then told him that is what I had come to do, and would he mind if I did it there? He told me, "No problem; go for it."

I positioned myself on the other side of the sidewalk, with eight or ten men on benches in front of me. Not knowing what to do next, I asked them if they would sing a verse of "Jesus Loves Me" with me. Much to my surprise, they did, and they sounded very good. This helped me gain a little confidence, so I brought them a sermon that I had prepared for such an occasion as this. It was on the imminent return of Christ and the signs of His coming. No sooner had I begun, when the one man who was sitting behind me got up and began looking over my shoulder at my Bible and notes, occasionally bumping me. This man was a big, young, husky guy, about half a head taller than me, and I believed he was trying to intimidate me, which he was successfully doing, even though he didn't know it. Not knowing what to do, I turned to him, and as privately as possible asked him if he could read. He immediately said that he could, so I just as quickly handed him my open Bible, telling him that every time I came to a verse that needed reading, he could do so. Pleasantly surprised, he said that he would. (I couldn't believe that I had just handed a perfect stranger my treasured Bible, not knowing for sure if he could be trusted with it.) It was not long before I came to a verse, and he did a great job of reading it with much expression, and a lot of finger pointing. I privately told him that while he was pointing one finger at them, there were three pointing back at him, and what he was reading applied just as much to him as it did to them. We continued to the end of the message, and I gave an invitation, which included the sinner's prayer.

If anyone responded to any part of the effort, I do not remember, but this one thing I do know: Even though we may not want to actually be a witness for Jesus, He will open doors that we would just as soon stay shut, and He will give us opportunities to witness for Him. What is decided is not my responsibility, but my obedience to the Master is.

CHAPTER 11

A Spirit-Changed Life

Twenty-five years ago, before this ministry was called *Sparrow Ministry*, I encountered a very frightful and intimidating man at the first rescue mission where I began speaking. I was a new preacher who was looking for opportunities to speak to lost adults, but with my lack of experience, I felt somewhat overwhelmed. Other preachers had said that to really be used by the Lord, we needed to leave our comfort zone, so there I was, way out of my comfort zone.

I encountered this frightful man on one of my first visits to this mission, and he was unlike any other person I had ever seen. I will try to share a word picture of what I saw. He was a tall, husky, muscular man with long, dirty hair with a few dreadlocks and facial hair in serious need of attention. His beard was matted with particles of food and perhaps small pieces of trash. I did not see anything alive and moving in his beard except a small portion of his face. As you might expect, his clothing was dirty and worn, little more than a collection of dirty rags. He did have an unusual feature: his eyes were dark and piercing, making it seem as though he could cut right through you with them. He was seated in the front row just in front of the pulpit, less than six feet away. The pulpit was a big, thick, heavy wooden one, and I was glad, thinking that it might afford a small degree of safety as a hiding place if needed. As I began speaking, I noticed that he was giving me his full attention, and it did not appear that he liked what I was saying. He looked unfriendly before I started, but now he appeared agitated, well on his way to being downright angry. He began another game of intimidation by subtly pointing his finger at me and waving it as if to say no to what I was saying. With difficulty, I tried to not think about him, and instead concentrate on the message that I had laboured over to prepare for them. As I continued, so did he, never letting up.

We finally made it to the altar call, and much to my surprise, several people responded, coming forward and praying to receive Jesus as their Lord and Savior. As we were leaving, I was glad that several people from our church were with me, including my wife Rebecca. You never know; I might have needed someone to protect me, or at least be able to say later on what had happened to me.

It was over, and I had survived for another day.

Because I was on their monthly schedule, I returned the following month, and to my surprise he was there again, at the same place, doing the same things. The only thing that had changed was that we were both a month older, but we were both just as determined. This time I was a little bit better prepared.

The Lord had given me a message of hope, acceptance, and love, and without speaking exclusively to him, I did look him right in the eyes as much as possible and speak from my heart to his. It was going much better for me this time, and I was feeling as though words were just flowing out of my mouth with power. At first, he was not receiving them well, but about halfway through, I noticed tears began to flow down his crusted face, disappearing into his shaggy beard. There was an amazing transformation in his countenance, as the hard look of anger had begun to leave, being replaced with sincere humility.

As I began to give the altar call, or invitation, he was one of the first to respond, with many others to follow. This was one of those HALLELUJAH! moments, as tears of joy were streaming down my face. I probably would have been shouting, "GLORY!" had it not been for my Baptist training. With the Bible telling us, *Likewise, I say unto you, there is joy in the presence of the angels of God over one sinner that repenteth* (Luke 15:10), we should rejoice with those who rejoice.

As we went home that evening, I felt like there was nothing to fear, then or ever, as long as I was living in His will, doing those things that He has allowed and called me to do. It gave real meaning to the verse: *Ye are of God, little children, and have overcome them: because greater is he that is in you, than he that is in the world* (1 John 4:4).

Upon returning to the mission the next month, I was looking for the man, wondering if there would be any signs of change in his life, but was disappointed that I did not see him. Then I noticed a man about his size that I thought looked somewhat familiar. When I saw his eyes, I knew it was the man I was looking for. His hair was neatly trimmed and clean, and there was no dirty beard or mustache. His clothing was clean and neat, and he seemed happy and content.

The change in him was evident to all. It was more than an idle proclamation that "I have Jesus"; he was becoming a reflection of the image of Christ.

For several months after that he was there, and he seemed glad to be. I have not seen him in years and never knew his name, but when I see him again, he will have a new name written in glory.

When the Lord changes a person, assuming there is a positive response to the calling of the Holy Spirit to the saving knowledge of Jesus, there is a lasting change. We should never let the devil scare us into submitting to him, because if we put on the armor of God, we can walk in victory.

Finally, my brethren, be strong in the Lord, and in the power of his might.

Put on the whole armour of God, that ye may be able to stand against the wiles of the devil.

For we wrestle not against flesh and blood, but against principalities, against powers, against the rulers of the darkness of this world, against spiritual wickedness in high places.

Wherefore take unto you the whole armour of God, that ye may be able to withstand in the evil day, and having done all, to stand.

Stand therefore, having your loins girt about with truth, and having on the breastplate of righteousness;

And your feet shod with the preparation of the gospel of peace;

Above all, taking the shield of faith, wherewith ye shall be able to quench all the fiery darts of the wicked.

And take the helmet of salvation, and the sword of the Spirit, which is the word of God:

Praying always with all prayer and supplication in the Spirit, and watching thereunto with all perseverance and supplication for all saints;

(Ephesians 6:10–18)

CHAPTER 12

Hot Hitchhiker Finds More Than a Ride to Hannibal

Having left home earlier than usual, traveling from Trenton to Peoria, Illinois, on the safest, easiest, and quickest route to Peoria, I was scheduled to speak at the rescue mission that evening. While traveling on US Highway 36, I realized that it would be lunchtime, and Brookfield had more to offer than any other town in the area. (Probably makes you wonder how I would know that.) Well, the taco salad was the most exciting bowl of lettuce that was available, so it was nibbled down and I hopped back into the *sparrowmobile* (keep eating like that and it will have to become the *bunny buggy*).

The point is that after lunch, it was back in the car to continue the trip. Entering the on-ramp to get back onto Highway 36, there was a tall man dressed in what I would call southwestern clothing, wearing a white, wide-brim hat, an off-white, short-sleeved, collared shirt, and denim jeans, complete with western boots. He was carrying a small backpack. It was quite obvious that he had somewhere to go and needed a little help getting there, so I pulled over before I got to him, rolled down the window, and asked him if he needed a ride. He did, so he put his bag in the back, while I moved mine out of the front seat, and he got in, taking off the big hat. He was very grateful to be in out of the sun and on the road again. The temperature was around one hundred degrees, with little or no wind blowing and no shade available, except for his hat. Perspiration was streaming down his forehead and face, so I turned the air conditioner on high and gave him a couple bottles of water, for which he again expressed his appreciation. This man did not seem like, or for that matter smell like, the average hitchhiker. He was articulate and well spoken, and upon asking him what his trade was, he told me that he was a writer for gun and western magazines, writing short stories about history and guns. He further described himself as a humorist, and I found he was a very interesting person to talk to.

After learning a bit about him, he asked if I was a preacher. I don't know if it was the Bible on the dash, or the Southern Gospel music that was playing when he got into the car that made him think that, because at that point I had not revealed the real reason I had invited him into the car. Since I was on my way to tell people in Peoria about the love of Jesus, I thought it would be fun to share the message of salvation with a wayfaring man. In our conversation, we compared stories of our times in the service. He spent twenty years in the US Marine Corps, and I was in the US Navy for four years. Somewhere in our conversation he mentioned that even though he was not a Christian, he believed some of the Bible. I listened to him talk for a little while and then interrupted him.

I told him that I did not understand what he meant, when he said he was not a Christian but still believed the Bible. If one knows what a Christian is, that would require one to know what he believes and why, and if one has that much information and truly believes any part of it, how could one resist believing all of it? Further, how would one know which part to believe, and which part not to believe? How could one know more about the Word than the one who penned it? He then told me that when he began to learn about science in college, he started doubting the Bible. I asked him how that could be, because the more you know about science, the more you would realize that everything is done in order, without random selection. I told him of the college course I had taken, "An Overview of Biology," where I was taught about the single cells of plants as compared to the single cells of animals. They both have all the same parts, except the plant cell has one additional ingredient, and that is chlorophyll, which has continued for six thousand years without a single change. If that were all the evidence of the divine Creator that was available, it should be enough, but that is just a very small and exact building block that all living things, both plant and animals, are made of. Then you must consider the multitude of different plants and animals, each containing the seed for the next generation, which grew from the seed of the generation before it, and never morphing into something different, but for all these years remaining the same. With that type of evidence, how could you possibly believe this was just a matter of chance?

Then I told him the story of the girl who was being raised by a mother and father who did not share the same beliefs. The mother taught the girl about creation and how she was made in the image and likeness of God. The dad claimed to believe that there is no God, and that it was random selection which directed the single cell into becoming an ape, eventually becoming a human. He was trying to persuade his daughter that this was the truth. She went to her mother one day, and asked her why her dad insisted that man came from an ape when she said that we are created. The mother finally told her daughter, "I am telling you about my side of the family, and your dad is talking about his." That story pretty much ended the discussion on creation compared to evolution, so we moved on.

Our time together was rapidly coming to a close. It was time for me to be bold and tell him that a lot of what he was telling himself was similar to what I claimed to believe before coming to the realization that if I were to die, I would have no hope of heaven, in case the Christians were correct. Then God allowed a series of events to occur in my life that illustrated to me that life was a temporary thing, and that almost half the amount of time I could expect to live had already passed. Why would God ever let me into heaven when I attempted to deny the very existence of Jesus? I continued by telling him of the friend who found me in my despair and told me of the love and forgiveness of Jesus – that He loved me before I was even born, and paid the price of my sins. All I needed to do was to believe that He was my only hope of heaven, as well as the Lord of my life. He had died, and God raised Him from the dead, and I was telling others of my faith in Him. He would save me, giving me everlasting life with Him. The hitchhiker didn't appear to be as sure of himself as he had been at the beginning of our conversation, and admitted that. We then discussed the brevity of time, and I shared the story of being terrorized by a headless chicken over sixty years ago, remembering it as though it were yesterday. Because of our own experience with time, we can therefore know that we are rushing toward the grave.

We had now run out of time and were sitting in the car at his destination in Hannibal, but he took the time to listen to the last reason why it was an urgent matter to be right with God before we meet Him face to face. I reminded him that he had said he was not a Christian, and I had said that I was, and then asked him what he thought I would lose if I died and discovered that there was no eternity. He told me that I would not lose anything, except for my hope of a future after death.

Then I asked him what he would lose upon dying and learning that he was wrong. After thinking about it briefly his reply was, "I would lose it all, because it would be too late." We were then completely out of time, and I had to leave, but before leaving, I encouraged him to accept Jesus as his hope of heaven and make Him the Lord of his life. Then I gave him a *Sparrow Ministry* songbook, which has the plan of salvation in it, including what Jesus would like to hear from us, or a version of what I call the sinner's prayer.

With that, I drove away, praying that the Spirit of God would continue to draw the hitchhiker to the saving knowledge of Jesus Christ, thereby giving him more than a ride down a highway in this life, but a ride to glory when Jesus comes again.

Perhaps he will choose Jesus as I did, some thirty-six years ago. Things have never been the same. If people only knew the joy of a believer, they would want what we have. We must share Jesus with others.

CHAPTER 13

Challenge of Spirits

Services that are scheduled just before lunch can be some of the most challenging to speak at for a number of reasons. It is soon obvious that the guests have not assembled to take part in a gospel-preaching, soul-searching, life-changing, Christ-honoring meeting. I strongly suspect that food, shelter, and rest is the main attraction, and by this time of day, discouragement and boredom have begun to set in, because this day seems to have no more promise of relief than the ones before. The day is markedly passing, and nothing is likely to change. Those who did not get enough rest in the night take advantage of being in a warm room with a chair to sit in. Often, the droning sound of a monotone speaker or a small airplane circling the runway, looking for a place to land, is more than their alert mode can endure, so they drift off into dreamy land, where things seem better for a time (kind of like this first paragraph).

As a frequent speaker, and knowing that this most likely will be the challenge, I must prepare by trusting the Lord to give me His message, trying to be a person the Lord can use, and being sure the "armor of God" is in place, because I am again entering into spiritual warfare, being involved as a soldier of the cross, a fisher of men.

On a typical day such as I just described, with a room of approximately one hundred guests, we started the meeting by singing a few songs together. It was actually starting out better than usual with quite a bit of participation, and they were singing great. Then a medium-size man, wearing a heavy, hooded coat and unusual barbecue mittens that were very flared where they began at his elbow, tapering to his hands, and carrying a bag about the size of a young, tightly wrapped baby (and handling it as though it were one). He came into the room. Making his way to one of the empty chairs in the front row, he sat right in front of me, his face less than six feet from mine.

It was easy for him to get this front seat, even though he was a little late, like it is at most churches where people gather at the back, next to the exit, in case there is a fire or something like that. His entry and dress, along with the way he was carrying the bag and where he sat, had attracted quite a bit of attention from all of us, perhaps even more than I was receiving. This was not half of the show.

He began rocking and bouncing his "baby" bag, talking quietly to it, patting and stroking it with his dirty mittens, occasionally laying it on his knees while holding up and waving "holy hands" in response to what I was saying. It is hard to say which was the most distracting, the imagined (I hope) child care or his alleged showy worship. It would be less than true for me to not say that I was having a great struggle trying to ignore all this, and give the rest of the congregation the attention they deserved. It was plain to see that they, understandably, were also trying hard to not be distracted. There were some positive things through it all: There were fewer sleepers and no one was snoring that I could hear.

With distractions almost forgotten again, the message was gaining momentum and heading for the victory lap, when I heard a big plop. He had thrown his baby bag down on the floor in front of me.

I kept speaking without missing a beat. Then with a look of remorse, he picked the bundle up and began rocking, patting, and talking to it more intensely than before. His big grab for everyone's attention had not worked.

As we came to the end of the service, I invited people to pray, asking Jesus to be their Savior and Lord of their life. Many men prayed aloud. Immediately upon ending that prayer, I told them that we were not quite finished. Apparently, even though I was not finished, they were, because many jumped up, heading for the door so they could be first in the chow line. This would not allow enough time for those who needed to stand in order to make their public profession for Christ. Once again I had a major distraction to deal with in this service. After a few seconds of wrangling, and a little stern speech, we finally regained order, resulting in more than ten people making public their decisions for Christ.

With the victory in Jesus, I completely lost track of the original distraction, not even seeing him leave. It is truly a great joy to be on the winning team.

> *Ye are of God, little children, and have overcome them: because greater is He that is in you than he that is in the world* (1 John 4:4).

Thank You, Jesus!

CHAPTER 14

Knocking on My Door

Because of the distance I am from home and the expense of travel accommodations, the Salina Rescue Mission has put together a suite for ministry guests. Several other missions where I speak also have facilities prepared for overnight ministry guests, and others will allow me to stay in the dorms for people in their recovery programs or with regular overnight guests. Most do not have a private bathing facility. It is very true that the older and more broken my body becomes, the more I appreciate privacy, especially while bathing, and the suite in Salina does include a private, fully equipped bathroom, along with a bedroom, living room, and foyer/game room, complete with a locking entrance door. The entire area is decorated with furniture that has been donated to the mission, and they have done a good job in using what they have to work with.

Now, I want to tell you about the mysterious knock at the door. First, it is necessary to tell you of its location and why I was behind it. I had taken my overnight bag and clothing into the room in the mission, shut the door, and was just starting to settle in after a long day and a challenging meeting with some big decisions for Christ. Frankly, I was thinking, *Do I rest in the living room, at the table and easy chairs in the foyer, or on the bed or couch in the bedroom?* They all looked very inviting, but before I had come to that decision, there seemed to be a muffled knock at the entrance door in the foyer. I wasn't even sure that it was my door. It was the last door at the end of a long hall, and there was no one on the other side of the hall that I knew of, so I opened the door.

There was no one at the door, and looking down the hall, I didn't see anyone. I did, however, notice the grey house cat sitting facing my open door, just looking in. I probably would have asked it in, but not knowing whether or not I should, and being the *fluffy sparrow*, you know birds usually don't get too cozy with unknown house cats. Well, all that I knew to do, since it appeared that the cat had knocked at my door, was to be neighborly, so I began talking to it, commending it for its ability to communicate with me by knocking at my door. As we were visiting, someone up the hall seemed to be amused about something because there was a little stifled laugh. About that time another amused person appeared from the other side of the hall. All the while, the cat continued to sit, looking through the open door to my room, and then looking at me, while we were discussing how the cat and two guys happened to all be in the hall at once.

I doubt they expected their cat trick to work so well. It sure had me fooled; I was convinced that the cat had just come and knocked at my door because it wanted to visit with me. The cat and I had made casual acquaintance on several occasions over a couple of years, and I did feel that we were somewhat okay with each other. I was pleasantly surprised to be accepted enough into the mission family to share in what developed into a classically funny situation with the cat playing its part as if it were rehearsed.

It makes me very thankful to all the participants in this story: Mission Director Reverend Steve Kmetz and the board of directors, for choosing to provide room for soldiers of the cross; the workers of the mission for accepting me as their brother; the cat, who has always acted like it wanted to be friends, if it only had the time; the overnight guests at the mission who feel free to talk to me; and last, those of you who make all these *sparrow flights* possible with your prayers and support.

I have tried to convey to you the surprise, joy, fun, laughter, kindness, and seriousness of this story as seen through my eyes and felt by my heart. To my knowledge, the only player that didn't experience humor was the cat. As we were laughing and talking about the trick and how well it worked, the cat decided to quit waiting and left the door. Walking past me, he lightly brushed my leg, continuing up the hall and looking back and saying, "Meow," as if to imply, "If you would have taken the time, we could have visited."

> Jesus tells us, *Behold, I stand at the door, and knock: if any man hear my voice, and open the door, I will come in to him, and will sup with him, and he with me* (Revelation 3:20).

Do I not recognize Jesus at my door and many times go rushing right past Him, not having the time to visit with Him, responding only to those things that are clamoring for my attention?

CHAPTER 15

Sunny, Warm Texas

A pastor friend of mine suggested that we go on a mission trip to Dallas, Texas, which was something I have wanted to do and had been looking into. While arranging my schedule to accommodate that, leaving most of the first week of each month open for such an occasion, we planned to go on this adventure the first week of February 2011.

Having noticed that a number of church members exit northern Missouri each winter and head for sunny Texas, I thought it made sense to learn from them and go that way, instead of going farther north or east. The time had come for me to realize my dream of a warmer climate.

That same week, though, I was scheduled to speak on Monday night in Denver, Colorado, at the Denver Rescue Mission. I had contacted several missions in the Dallas-Fort Worth area, and actually had a couple of appointments to speak to chapel volunteer coordinators and was excited to have the opportunity to do this. It would not be a problem to come back through Missouri to pick up Pastor Ron Adrian, which is what I planned to do.

That Monday afternoon, as I was arriving in Denver, there was something else arriving also: a fierce winter storm. The temperature began to drop and the wind howled while moisture in various forms began to fall. The highways began to be like giant parking lots as things really got slick, causing a number of fender benders. Reports were that this was a mammoth storm stretching from the mountains in Colorado east through Illinois, starting in a line across Texas into Arkansas, going north through all of Missouri. In other words, everywhere I intended to travel would be covered by a blanket of snow and ice, with subzero temperatures and dangerous winds, causing many roads to be closed. If I planned to keep my appointments in Dallas, returning to Missouri on the way to Dallas was out of the question.

After completing the two back-to-back services in Denver, and witnessing more than twenty-five people make decisions for Jesus Christ, and while the winter storm was still raging, I headed south. The new plan was to go south to a point, then go east, straight into Dallas, and avoid some of the storm. While it seemed to be a good plan to me, God had other plans. Another problem was meager finances, since all the expenses would now be paid by *Sparrow Ministry*, and I knew there would not be enough for four nights of motel bills, along with the fuel and food. What was I going to do? It embarrasses me that at the slightest hint of a problem, I forget such powerful promises as:

> *Trust in the LORD with all thine heart; and lean not unto thine own understanding. In all thy ways acknowledge him, and he shall direct thy paths* (Proverbs 3:5–6).

> *Let your conversation be without covetousness; and be content with such things as ye have: for he hath said, I will never leave thee, nor forsake thee* (Hebrews 13:5).

Take therefore no thought for the morrow: for the morrow shall take thought for the things of itself. Sufficient unto the day is the evil thereof (Matthew 6:34).

These verses are easy to quote to others, but sometimes difficult to accept when walking by sight instead of by faith. I ask myself, *Why would you ever doubt God, Earl? He has never let you down.* As I look back, I cannot see my skeletal remains. The Lord always provides, so what was the problem with this new set of challenges?

Having driven until I really needed some rest, it was now almost midnight, eight below zero, and the wind still blowing. There was a motel with a room for thirty-two dollars, and I had enough for one night's stay but had hoped not use it this soon. Reasoning with myself (not always a good thing to do), I thought that there may not be a tomorrow for me if I got caught out in this killer cold weather, so I should invest in a room now while I could. It would probably be warmer tomorrow.

It was still eight below Tuesday morning, but there was one change: the wind had picked up, causing the wind chill to be even more dangerous. I had made some preparations for this eventuality by having with me a propane catalytic heater with several fuel cells, a big wool blanket that my sister Nancy made (making me promise that I would keep it in my car), as well as a big down-filled coat with a hood, and plenty of snack foods. Leaving Colorado Springs, heading south to the corner of New Mexico, then going east toward Dallas, conditions did not improve. The roads were still awful with everything that had fallen now frozen solid. As I turned toward Dallas, the wind was blowing new snow across the road. It looked as though the snow was falling horizontally instead of vertically, but there was more accumulating on the road. Visibility was greatly diminished, and the landscape looked very desolate, with no houses or businesses visible as I traveled for many miles. Morning soon became afternoon, and I began to wonder if I would find fuel for the car in time.

During all this, I began to feel sorry for myself, and was talking to God about what I thought to be a deplorable situation, even shedding a few tears about the prospect of spending the next three nights in my mini camper, otherwise known as a Pontiac Montana van. I call it a mini camper because it sounds like I'm a vagrant if I say I'm sleeping in my car. While all this was going on in my mind, it was as if Jesus spoke to me saying, *"Earl, during my ministry in Israel, there were winters there. I did not have a home or a car with a heater or windows, and no wool blanket, yet I survived to make your salvation possible. Won't you enter with Me into the joy of sacrifice so that others might hear of Me and choose eternal life over eternal damnation?"* This was very startling to me, causing my self pity to turn into the joy of walking with the Lord. At that point I didn't even want a room, because God had given me everything that I needed, and everything would be all right, and it was.

The roads and weather got worse, and my attitude got better. My anticipation of seeing what the Lord was about to do in Dallas grew to a fever pitch, where I could hardly wait to see what was going to happen. My first appointment was canceled because the person I was to see did not make it to work due to the weather. The person I had the next appointment with forgot that I was coming, but he did come in and we went to lunch. While talking about *Sparrow Ministry* and my intentions, he told me that I could speak at the chapel service that very evening. God really does open doors and arrange schedules. I spoke that evening, witnessing more than forty precious souls make decisions for Jesus Christ, twenty-five accepting Jesus as

Savior, and more than fifteen re-dedicating their lives to Him. Wow! Thank you, Jesus!

Leaving Dallas and heading for home, I had a joyful heart from having followed through, doing what Jesus had given me to do, and especially because it was not easy or convenient. God must have been smiling, knowing that I had chosen Texas for my convenience more than for my concern for souls, so He arranged for an adjustment of my attitudes and priorities. The roads were even worse all the way into Kansas, but I now viewed that as the devil trying to cause me to think that it was not worth it. It only caused me to be more determined to press forward for the cause of Christ.

Won't you also consider stepping out of your comfort zone for the cause of Christ, if you have not already? He will bless your heart beyond measure, and build your faith as you witness Him helping you do the unlikely and that which is inconvenient.

CHAPTER 16

Terrorized by a Headless Chicken

It was a sunny afternoon at our place in southeast Kansas in the big town of Thayer (the size of the town measured by the legs of a four-year-old). While playing out in our yard, a traumatizing event occurred that I would not soon forget.

Our place was two city lots wide and half a block long. Highway 169, a north-south two-lane concrete road was the east boundary of our spread. The south boundary included some bushes, a long grape vine, a rhubarb patch growing in a couple of big tires filled with dirt, and an open space continuing to an outhouse. (It was possibly the strongest one in town, and not just the smell; it was made of big rocks and cement so kids couldn't turn it over on Halloween.) The outhouse sat on the southwest corner. Going west from there down the alley was a chicken house, formerly our home, until Dad finished building our big three-room house. The big was only in the eyes of this little boy. On the north end of the chicken house there was the chicken pen, about the same size as the chicken house, and at the north end of the pen there was a big stump in the ground that I will call the killing stump, clearly in view of our entire yard. The alley continued a ways farther north to a rock-covered street on the north side of our house, which then continued on to the highway. On this north side, there was a long garden that started at the alley and ended at the highway. Our big house was about a third of the length of the garden, set closer to the highway than the alley.

To understand the traumatic event that occurred, it is necessary to somewhat understand the lay of the land. That part of town was all pretty much flat, especially our place.

I have no idea what the occasion was, but while I was playing in the yard, over on the south side by the rhubarb patch, my mom came out the back door of our house where the kitchen was, went to the chicken house, and got a chicken. I hadn't been paying much attention until the chicken started squawking and flopping its wings, trying to escape, but I knew from personal experience that when Mom got ahold of you, there was no escaping. I didn't know what she was going to do with the chicken, but it didn't take long to find out. She did something that caused the chicken to lose its head. I think she chopped it off on the big stump (there was a hatchet stuck in it). She was holding it, and the bird flopped or something, but anyway, it got away, landing on its feet, with blood pumping out of its neck. The headless chicken began running – and it was running straight at me! In shock, I watched it coming, but it wasn't slowing down, so I took off running away from it and have never stopped, at least in my mind.

My only sister Nancy is two years older than I am. We have brothers that are older than she is, so she has always been my guardian (she thinks boss), protecting me from all harm. She has told me that when I took off running toward the highway, she was trying to catch me, and finally did. I was crying, and she eventually calmed me down, explaining the process of how fried chicken ended up on my plate.

I liked the chickens, because they were fun to watch and would usually talk to me, even though I was never able to learn their language. Fried chicken was always a favorite of mine also, perhaps preparing me for the ministry, but until that day, I had never considered the cost of it. As I recall, I didn't want any fried chicken for a while. It kind of seemed like I was eating a friend. I have since learned that if I do not become personally acquainted with the chickens or know their names, they taste a lot better.

That was more than sixty-four years ago. Where has the time gone? I remember it as though it happened this morning!

> The Bible tells me, *Whereas ye know not what shall be on the morrow. For what is your life? It is even a vapour, that appeareth for a little time, and then vanisheth away* (James 4:14).

Because of the seemingly short time ago that the headless chicken began chasing me, and my vivid memory of it since then, I cannot doubt the truth of that verse. Knowing that the average age of death is in the mid-seventies, I have to know that I am much closer to the grave than I am to the cradle. It is becoming increasingly evident to me that whatever I intend to do or need to do in this life, I better get on with it, because I am running out of steam (vapour).

You also are running out of time. So I ask you, Have you decided where you want to spend eternity, and have you acted on that decision? The choice is yours, and yours alone, because God loves you so much that He will not let anyone else make the choice for you. Several places in the Bible inform us what we must do to avoid an eternity in hell, spending it in heaven instead, but it requires a choice on our part.

CHAPTER 17

Tragedy in Texas

On my way to tell people how much Jesus loves them, this message was put to an individual face-to-face test of authority. It was a little like the story of the woman approaching Jesus at the well in Samaria, with the biggest difference being that I am just a representative of Jesus, and those of you who partner with me. The encounter occurred at a very busy gas station in east Texas.

It was mid-morning on a beautiful day as I was on my way to talk to the chapel speaker coordinator at the Highway 80 Rescue Mission in Longview, Texas, about the possibility of becoming one of their volunteer chapel speakers. Still having less than fifty miles to go, I was shocked to discover the little blinking gas pump light on the dash panel, attempting to notify me of an impending problem: Either get some gasoline very soon or walk. (Don't you just love those warning lights placed in cars for clueless people? Kinda makes me wonder why on earth they would put one in my car. Perhaps there is a message about warnings there.)

I stopped at the very next station, after praying that there would be one in time. Pulling up to a pump with a sigh of relief, I began to fill the tank with "liquid gold," and in the meantime, wash a few

Texas bugs from the windshield. (Yes, everything is bigger in Texas, even the bugs.) While finishing the window-cleaning job, I noticed a casually and modestly dressed woman, perhaps in her early thirties (they all look so young if they are fifty-something or less), with a little piece of paper in hand with something written on it, who apparently wanted to talk to me. I stopped to hear what she had to say, and she asked me if I would like to have her phone number. Even though I was born at night, it wasn't last night, so my response was, "Well, uh, why would I want your phone number?" She then asked me if I ever looked on *craigslist*, which I had to admit that once I was looking to buy a used camper van, so I looked there but didn't find anything I could afford. I wanted to know why she asked. She then told me that her name was on it and that I might want to call her sometime.

Looking straight into her pretty brown eyes that reminded me of two of my beautiful brown-eyed granddaughters, who also have rich brown hair as she had, I wondered what had gone so seriously wrong in her life to bring her to this. I told her that I would not be calling her and was not interested in what she had to offer. She then apologized, turned, and started walking away. I was left standing there, surprised and saddened by this encounter, because I had offered her nothing that could even encourage her or help her escape this life choice, and I didn't know what to do but just stand there. I felt compelled to do something, but by now she was at least two car lengths away, and this was a busy place. I finally said loudly, "Jesus loves you as much as He loves me or anyone else!" This statement had an immediate and unexpected effect.

She stopped, turned around, and walked back toward me. As she got close enough, I could see tears streaming down her face, and she told me that Jesus could not love her, and she was going to go to hell because of what she was doing, including drugs. Then, assuring her that Jesus really did love her, even though He knew what she was doing, because He tells us in His Word, *But God commendeth [proved] his love toward us, in that, while we were yet sinners, Christ died for us* (Romans 5:8), I also told her, *If we confess our sins, He is faithful and just to forgive us our sins, and to cleanse us from all unrighteousness* (1 John 1:9). She was having a difficult time accepting this because, in her words, she was so bad. We talked about all sins having the same results regarding our relationship with God, and where they would lead us, and the God-given remedy for them. I assured her that God was powerful enough to do for her what He said He would. What would be required of her would be to humbly accept Jesus as her Lord and Savior. At this point, she told me that she was already saved and had been saved four times.

To go further, this problem had to be cleared up, so we discussed the new birth being like our physical birth. Somewhere in our conversation, she had told me of a daughter that had been taken away from her and was adopted by one of her grandmothers. I asked her if her daughter was still her daughter, even though she was in the custody of someone else, or was there anything that could ever change the fact that she was the girl's birth mother? She said there was nothing that could ever take that away from her. I then asked her if she thought she was more powerful than God, and she admitted that she wasn't. Then we looked at John 10:28–29, where Jesus states: *And I give unto them eternal life, and they shall never perish, neither shall any man pluck them out of my hand. My Father, which gave them me, is greater than all; and no man is able to pluck them out of my Father's hand.* She then realized that she was saved as a teenager, and had re-committed her life to Jesus three other times, and was currently not living for Him.

Standing there at the gas pump for well over twenty minutes, we exchanged many words as she tried to justify why she was actually a good person who had been an active follower of Jesus, a Sunday school teacher, singer, and a lot of other things, causing us to look at Ephesians 2:8–9: *For by grace are ye saved through faith, and that not of yourselves: it is the gift of God: Not of works, lest any man should boast.* Her phone had been ringing every few minutes, and at one point a man in his twenties came over and said something to her. She told him to get back in the car and stay there, and clearly, she was torn between two worlds, the peace and rest that she knew existed with Jesus, and the lure of money the world had to offer. Throughout this encounter, she at times was sobbing in torment. All along her tears continued to flow, but she was not willing to let Jesus do a work in her life at that time.

I tried to convince her that she could find rest and safety at the women's shelter at the mission, but she didn't want to go there because there were too many drug users and sinners there. I was not sure if she thought she would be a bad influence on them, or they on her, but I did not ask. She was getting really fidgety and her phone wouldn't stop ringing, so I told her one last thing to consider. I asked her to take a good look in the mirror, and she would see a beautiful girl with a good complexion, clear bright eyes, healthy, straight teeth, and healthy, long, wavy hair. But if she continued on the road she claimed to be on, probably within three years, if she was still alive, she would be reduced to such a broken person that her hope of big money would all be gone.

She said that she would like to have a Bible, and *Sparrow Ministry* was able to provide her with a Bible, as well as a smaller New Testament. Again, she wanted me to take her phone number and call her to talk, and once again, I assured her that I would not be calling. I asked her, however, whether she would give me an address where she could receive mail, and I would write to her. I pray that she receives this story and considers the love and cleansing power of the Lord Jesus Christ. We prayed together before she left, and as she was walking away, I reminded her that the Bible tells us that he (or she) that knoweth to do good and doeth it not, to him it is sin.

I am not in the judging business, but the Bible tells us that we can know what kind of a tree we are by looking at the fruit we are bearing, and if we say that we have faith, and that faith is just talk, it is not worth anything. Fact is, many times people treat Jesus like some kind of a date they might flirt with for a while but do not want to have a personal relationship with, but then they still expect Him to be waiting to take the scraps at the end of their life and cherish them as though they were something special.

If we would believe and accept Jesus, letting Him be the Lord (master) of our life, He would take the pieces and make something very special out of them. The "Tragedy in Texas" is the true account of a life that has such great potential but is being wasted by choosing to live in what God calls sin.

CHAPTER 18

How God Can Turn Problems Into Blessings

Salina, Kansas, is one of the first rescue missions I called when Rebecca and I decided to go to more places than just City Union Mission in Kansas City, Missouri, to take the message of salvation through Jesus Christ to other homeless people. Salina has, for the most part, been a fun place to go, where we've seen many people make life-changing decisions for the Lord, and where we have also become acquainted with many of the mission's friendly and helpful staff, as well as meeting a most interesting house cat.

While there in June of 2011, the power to all of the gadgets that are plugged into the twelve-volt system of our mini camper stopped working. After the service, I went to the big, lighted parking lot of the local Walmart to see what the problem was. Being a former "shade tree mechanic," it seemed that it would be an upgrade to move to a paved, lighted parking lot to do repairs, not to mention how much more professional it would appear. After checking each fuse on the car with a tester and finding that they were all good, I tested the outlet in the car, discovering that it also worked. Upon testing the GPS – without which I probably would be perpetually lost, never being able to even find my way home – I plugged it directly into the outlet, bypassing the connector that has three outlets, and praise God! it worked, thereby identifying the connector as the problem. I started into Wally World to get a new one, and then decided that there was more testing to be done before spending money on a different one. A lesson I learned a long time ago as a mechanic is, you can't break something that is already broken, so I began to disassemble (a much better way to say it than "tear apart") the adapter. After a few pieces, I came across a little glass thing with two metal ends on it and a broken or burnt wire running through the middle of it. Well, perhaps the source of the problem was a burnt-out inline fuse. Again, off to the store (makes it kinda handy to have your repair facility right out in front of the store) to buy a little fuse. Have you ever tried to buy one fuse? The smallest package available is a package of ten or more. Using one fuse every five years, I doubt that I would use them all. After putting the new fuse in, plugging everything back in, and making sure that it was all working, it was time to celebrate by going to "Mickey D's" to party with a cup of decaf coffee.

Since McDonald's has free wireless Internet connection available, I took the net pad in with me to check emails and catch up on the news. The celebration took a little longer that I had intended, realizing that it was almost ten o'clock. Knowing that the Salina Rescue Mission locks their front door at 10:00 p.m., I hurriedly left the Arches and headed for the mission where I was staying for the night, before going to Wichita the next day. In the darkness, apparently not paying close enough attention to what I was doing, or where I was driving, and going the thirty-five miles per hour that was posted, all at once I saw a curb across the lane that I was in. Not having time to stop, and with no other traffic on southbound 9th Street, I swerved hard to the left, trying to miss the end of it. Next, there was a big bump and a swishing sound, soon followed by the flopping of a flat tire. There was no good place to pull off the road at that point, so I continued slowly to a Casey's station just down the road. Looking at the tire, it had a large hole torn in the side of it where I had bounced it off the curb. There would be no airing it up, or repairing it, so I took the spare tire from under the car and was taking the blown tire off, when a nice young man in a pickup truck, on his way back to college from a weekend at home, asked if he could help me. First I thought, *Why would he offer to help me? I have done this many times before for others.* Then on considering that I am now a tired old man, so *fluffy* and stiff that it is hard to bend over that far, and I didn't even have the car jacked up as yet, I thought again, and told him, "Yes, it would be a big help." The spare didn't have much air in it, so I got the trusty emergency pump out and started pumping. Finally the pressure came up to almost 30 psi, not anywhere close to the 60 psi that it needed. He put it on the car, lowered the jack, and watched it settle very close to the rim that was on the pavement. The station's tire pump was across the parking lot, so I carefully tried to get the car over there, and as I was turning, I heard that unpleasant sound of an Amish one-iron-wheeled buggy going down the road. Actually, I have never heard of this, but if there was ever such a thing, it would have sounded like this car with the metal rim running on the concrete drive. Upon arriving at the pump, hoping to get enough air to pick the car up, my hopes turned to despair. The pump had a note taped to it which simply stated, "Out of Order."

This was now the time to pause and reflect on my new situation; after all, I was not going to go anywhere anytime soon. First, I was thankful to have enough provisions to finish the remainder of this mission trip, including enough for the purchase of a new tire. Second, I wasn't sure what I should do, because the mission was several miles away and it was now after hours. There was no place at that time of day to get a tire fixed, even if I could get there. I called the mission and told them my tale of woe and joyfully listened to their response. They told me that they would come and get me, which they promptly did. The problem was not close to being solved, because now I was several miles away from the car, and it still had a flat tire with no spare tire.

Morning came, and I asked a friend if there might be anyone who could take me to the car, and he stopped what he was doing and said, "Let's go." We went to the car, got the blown tire, and headed off to Walmart. We took the tire into their shop, went to the counter, and asked the clerk the price of an equivalent tire, one without the hole. She came back in a few minutes with a printout of three tires: good, better, and best, to be interpreted as expensive, more expensive, and high-priced. As I was looking at the differences, trying to decide which would be the best value, my friend said, "We will take two of those," while pointing at the high-priced ones. In the meantime, he had taken out his wallet and a piece of magic plastic to pay for them. The lady would not let him pay for a second tire in advance, so we got the one, took it back to the car to put it on, and he insisted on putting it on, so I sacrificially yielded. With that done, we headed once again to my outdoor repair area to get the other tire. I parked the car back next to the tire shop. My friend decided to inspect the other tires, and he decided that they should all be replaced. I usually take tires further than they were intended to go but did not argue with him. After all, I have spoken to him about being a part of our advisory board, because I believe he would be of great value.

The end of the story and moral of it is: My friend replaced all the tires on the *sparrowmobile* with the best that Walmart had to offer, along with a road hazard warranty. (Wonder where he got that idea!)

My problem became a tremendous blessing. Thank you very much, my friend, and I pray that God will continue to bless you.

> *Trust in the LORD with all thine heart; and lean not unto thine own understanding. In all thy ways acknowledge him, and he shall direct thy paths* (Proverbs 3:5–6).

CHAPTER 19

Distressed Young Lady

With the heat index well over one hundred degrees, it was a scorching hot July evening in the downtown area of Kansas City, Missouri, even at eight o'clock at night. Tom, Dean, and I had just stepped out of City Union Mission after conducting a well-attended, as well as spiritually productive, evening chapel service. Perhaps our most important heavenly assignment of the day, however, was yet to present itself.

Dean and I had ministered at that rescue mission many times before, usually with our wives, but they were not with us this evening. This was the first time Tom was a part of our evangelistic team. Over twenty-six years ago, while on the pastoral staff at Blue Ridge Baptist Temple, the Lord impressed upon me to look beyond the pre-teenage children with whom I had been working and seek out a group of adults with whom I could share God's Word. The likelihood of having an opportunity to preach to adults was very slim in that I was the fourth or fifth person in line on the pastoral staff, and all wanted the opportunity to preach. Not content to just stand by and wait, I contacted the mission asking whether I could speak at one of their many chapel services, seeing that they had at least two services a day at the men's shelter. After being approved as one of their many speakers, I talked to James Ogan, Dean Johnson, and several others about forming a ministry team to minister at City Union Mission, as well as other places. Dean and Marian have faithfully continued to partner with Rebecca and me over these many years. Dean has led the gospel singing for about half of this time. Enough about what led us to this day; now on with the story.

We saw a police van pull to the curb as it was traveling north on Troost, about half a city block from the mission, and a young woman got out of the front passenger side and began walking toward us. All she had with her was the clothing on her back: a sleeveless T-shirt, some modest shorts that came almost to her knees, sandals, and a small bag. She was clean and neat, with no makeup or jewelry on, looking like she might have dressed for a church picnic or to watch a sporting event.

As she walked up to us, she asked if we knew where City Union Mission was. Because she was so close to the door, she could not see past the permanent awning over our heads where the sign was, so I told her that she was there. She then asked if this was a women's shelter. I hated to tell her that it wasn't, but the women's part was just a couple of miles away. She tried to mask her disappointment, but the tears forming in her eyes betrayed her true emotions. Trying to comfort her, I assured her that we would find some help somewhere, but she obviously found very little comfort in that statement. By now we were back in the building where it was cooler, and standing by the check-in desk (where she could not check in), and some kind person offered her a cup of water, which she gladly took. Upon asking her if she had anything to eat that day, she said that she had not. Another kind worker at the mission went to get her some food. While we were waiting for the worker's return, she asked if she could sit down, because she was really tired.

In trying to find out a little about her without making it seem like the Great Inquisition, I asked her if she was older or younger than twenty. She said she was nineteen years old. Then I inquired whether she had any family in Kansas City, and her response was that she was living with her father, but they didn't get along very well, so she had left home, apparently some time that day. Since my mission is to try to draw people to a closer relationship with Jesus, I asked her if she had any religious background. She told me that she had, that her mother was a Jew, and that she and her mother had also attended a Nazarene church. Then in asking her if she knew Jesus as her personal Savior, she said that she did. Since I enjoy hearing people's personal testimonies, I asked if she would share hers with me. She began by telling me that she was saved when she was three years old. That being such a remarkable age to realize one's sinfulness and need for salvation, I then asked her if that was an occasion that she actually remembered, or did she just remember someone telling her about what she had done. She responded by telling me that she, in fact, remembers the time, even though she had not always lived as she should. Further, she desired to have a renewed relationship with the Lord. Since she never spoke of her mother again, I assumed that her mother was no longer in the picture for whatever reason, and it would be best for me to not ask about her. Understanding a little bit more about her situation, we then proceeded in attempting to find the girl shelter for the night.

Deciding that I should call the homeless hotline, I got them on the phone, and the person whom I was speaking to told me there were no shelter beds for any more women in Kansas City this night. Not willing to accept that, I told her of the desperate situation with this young lady. While on the phone with "Hotline for the Homeless," two different overnight guests at the men's shelter tried to get the girl to let them take her in their car to a shelter they knew of. I thanked them but told them no, that she would be provided for. One man did not want to give up, but after a few more words, decided to go his way. When the lady from the hotline overheard our interruption, she told me to hold on while she made another call. In less than a minute she was back with good news that the ladies' shelter of City Union Mission had a cot that she could sleep on in a safe room. I told her that we would be there within fifteen minutes. Tom, the young lady, and I got in the *sparrowmobile* to take her to the other shelter.

There was one little problem in that I usually only have two seats in the van, and we needed three. Tom volunteered to sit on the floor in the back, making a place for the girl in the front, so we headed out. I thought I knew where the other shelter was, but gave up before wasting any time. I pulled over, set the GPS, and found that we were about a block away, just around the corner.

On the short trip over there, the young lady told us that she wanted to get back into fellowship with the Lord. I reminded her of the words in 1 John 1:9 where we are told: *If we confess our sins, he is faithful and just to forgive us our sins, and to cleanse us from all unrighteousness,* and that included her. No matter what had led to her situation, the problem was not too big for the Lord. She needed to give it to Him, and follow the lead of the Holy Spirit, letting the Lord have control of her life. I think that she did believe those words, because she began to seem a little less distressed, and perhaps somewhat relaxed. She then said that she wanted to have a Bible and wanted us to pray for her before she went into the mission. I most always have several Bibles in the van, so I gave her one that had been given to me. We were now at the mission and got out and joined hands in a small circle of prayer for her safety and future, as well as for her spiritual growth.

I went in with her to make sure she did have a safe place for the night, and the lady at the check-in was expecting her. We all know that is not the end of her story, but we will probably have to wait for heaven to know the ending. Please, let's all lift this unnamed, lovely, young lady up in prayer, along with the thousands of other homeless people who are in great peril. God has His eye on them all, along with the homeless sparrows.

CHAPTER 20

Hot Night in East Texas

The Lord recently impressed upon one of our partners in ministry the possibility of purchasing a full-size Dodge van to travel in, and it is really a blessing. It would be like comparing a small one-room studio apartment to a house with a bedroom, living room, and work area. The back seat folds down into a bed that is large enough to stretch out on for a comfortable night's rest. This is made possible by two strategically placed windows. These windows allow me to lay with my feet almost against one, and my head against the other. If I get any taller, it will be a problem, but it seems that nowadays, all my growth just makes me fluffier.

Now that the Dodge is available and is so user friendly, I enjoy using it most of the time. I was traveling in it on the last trip from Dallas to Shreveport, and since I got out of Dallas after 9:00 p.m., I stopped at a restaurant for supper (that would be "dinner" for city folks), followed by a couple of hours of writing. Upon leaving the restaurant and driving on toward my next destination, I decided to stop for the night about midnight. Even though it was still over one hundred degrees outside, I decided to open all the windows, lean the driver's seat back, and get a little rest.

The breeze I hoped for did not materialize, so it was getting very hot. I had made the mistake of getting an indoor-outdoor thermometer, so if there was ever any question of how miserable it was, I could know for sure. Checking this device that was capable of accurately measuring one's level of discomfort, I was surprised to see that it was only 110 degrees. It felt much hotter than that. It was hot enough that I really felt sorry for those who had once again rejected the message of salvation, instead choosing to take their chances on hell with its eternal flames.

Speaking of decisions, it was time for me to make one before I was scorched. I was beginning to think that I could smell bacon cooking, and my shirt was wet, but it sure wasn't rain. Texas had a lot of wildfires because it was so hot and dry.

By now, it was after 1:00 a.m., certainly too late to waste money on a motel room. Upon appraising the situation, I decided that a different location would probably be better than that truck stop parking lot. It was in a low spot with a lot of wind brakes, and even though there was enough breeze to ruffle the leaves in the surrounding trees, there was none getting to me. The road in front of the truck stop led off to the south on higher ground, so I drove down it a couple of miles into the country, and came to a country church with a fair-sized, partially paved parking lot and a couple of houses across the road from it. It seemed like a perfect place for a tired traveler to get some rest. Since it was a Baptist church, and that is my brand, I felt perfectly welcome there. So this time I opened all the doors, as well as the windows, imagined that there was a cool breeze (so much for positive thinking; it was still quite warm), leaned the seat back, shut my eyes, took a few deep breaths, and drifted off to sleep.

Waking about an hour later with a start, I thought I heard someone holler, "HEY!" I sat up straight, looking all around, and even though there was a little light, I could not see or hear anything out of the ordinary besides the buzzing in my ears. Thinking that I probably just imagined that someone had called out, I lay back and drifted back to sleep. Soon I was definitely hearing some voices, and they seemed to be getting closer. It seemed odd that anyone would be walking on the road at this time of night, but as the voices continued and were getting closer, it was time for me to sit up and take notice. This time it was real, because I was starting to make out someone or someones walking directly toward the van.

I didn't know what to do, so I quietly waited to see what was next. I believe the Scripture that tells me to *Trust in the LORD with all thine heart; and lean not unto thine own understanding. In all thy ways acknowledge him, and he shall direct thy paths* (Proverbs 3:5–6). I knew that I was on a mission for the Lord, and even though He did not tell me to sleep in this parking lot, He had not directed me not to, so I would just sit tight and see how this all played out.

There were two older men walking toward me, and as they got closer, I could see that they both had something in their hands. One had some kind of walking stick, and the other one had a stick and some kind of lever-action gun. In the darkness, I couldn't tell if it was a rifle, shotgun, or perhaps just a BB gun, but it was definitely a gun, and I did not want to find out how big of a bullet it might have in it. I had a slight advantage over them, because I could see them better than they could see me, so they had no idea what I might have in my hands. One of them spoke first, asking what I was doing there. I responded by telling them that I was just trying to get a little rest, that I was a traveling preacher who had spoken at a mission in Dallas, and was now on my way to Shreveport and thought I had found a quiet place to rest. The one without the gun was doing the talking, and he said that there had been some break-ins around there, so they came to check me out. Then he said that he had been looking down that way and he saw someone walking around my van, and he had hollered, and they ran down toward the church. They asked me a few more questions, and then the one without the gun walked around the church, seeing if anything had been broken into. Finding nothing, he came back to us. They began asking more questions and seemed to be getting a little angry, so I told them that we could settle this right now. I would just call the law, and they could come out and check us all out, and we could live happily ever after. At that point, they must have decided that we had talked long enough, or perhaps they finally believed me, so they walked away into the night.

After they left, I got out and closed all the doors, started the van, and drove slowly away, so as not to disturb them any more than they already had been; after all, they still had the gun. Even though I can drive fast, I probably cannot match or exceed the velocity of even a fired BB.

I do enjoy evangelism, and enjoyed the victory of witnessing twenty-six people make decisions for Jesus that night, so I was not ready to give the devil a victory in scaring me. Truly, life with the Lord is an excellent adventure, made for us to enjoy.

We are told in His Word: *And the peace of God, which passeth all understanding, shall keep your hearts and minds through Christ Jesus* (Philippians 4:7).

CHAPTER 21

Warm Breath from God

This day was another of those scorching-hot summer days in east Texas, with the temperature well over one hundred degrees. It had been this hot for more than thirty days in a row. The Lord has continued to pour out the very thing that caused me to want to come to Texas in the first place: much more heat than I had wanted or expected. My search should have been based on concentrations of lost souls first, instead of my personal comfort; however, in confusion, I chose to go to Texas, first for warmer weather, and second to find a few lost souls for Jesus so as to justify the trip.

Previously, I wrote about my first missionary trip to Texas when I experienced several inches of ice on the road as well as on everything else, and temperatures near zero and below. Spending a few days in this deep freeze caused me to make a cool calculation. This was that I realized my motive for being in Texas was not what it should have been, and this extreme cold or heat for several months in a row was not going to put me in any kind of comfort zone, so I must forget about my comfort and concentrate on telling people about Jesus, whether the weather is hot, cold, or somewhere in between.

While traveling from Shreveport to Dallas, it was over 110 degrees most everywhere except on the highways, which yielded a temperature of over 120 degrees, but I found a cool place to spend the middle of the day. The Golden Arches is a favorite place of mine, because their air conditioners usually work, and they are not afraid to use them. This day I had plenty of time to enjoy their comfort.

After a big bowl of lettuce with a few trimmings that probably would have put a big smile on the face of any Texas jackrabbit, I was settling into making phone calls, which caused me to return to the hot van to get the address and phone book, appointment book, school book, notebook, and Bible.

Upon completing the necessary phone calls, it was time to work on my continuing, on-going, never-ending education. If I didn't get busy and make the grade, I probably would never get the big raise as a missionary evangelist. Sometimes I forget that my contract is with the Lord and it goes kind of like this: "IF I serve Him, He will take care of all my needs. I am NOT to worry about the details." Since the Lord never asked to see my résumé, He is not likely to be impressed with another degree more or less. Success with Him is not in what we learn about doing, but what we actually get up and do, whether we have been bona fide authorized or qualified in man's opinion or not.

The portion of Scripture that I had been pondering and writing a paper on was John 4:45–54, where John tells of a nobleman's son being healed. In the revelation section of that paper, I had come to the conclusion that the longer I trust Jesus, the more I realize the many places He intercedes for me and protects me from harm.

Looking at the clock, it was time to move on toward Dallas. I hurriedly picked up the trash, putting it on the tray, and stacked up the books with the largest on the bottom and the smallest on the top, which is the appointment/calendar book. It is wire-bound with a thick, plastic, laminated, cardboard cover, about four by eight inches in size. There were two unused napkins that I couldn't throw away, so I placed them under the cover of the top book, wondering if I would ever find them again.

With the stack of books under one arm and a cold drink in the other hand, I walked out into what felt like a convection oven with the fan running. I noticed that it had not cooled off. I had to set something down so I could get the keys to unlock the van and open the door. I set the stack of books on the roof, opened the door, got in, put the drink in a holder, and then started the van while turning on the air. It had to be well over 130 degrees in the vehicle, and the sooner it got moving, the sooner it would cool off. With the van started and the air trying to work, I fastened the seatbelt, put it in gear, and started to back out of the parking place.

Out of the corner of my eye I noticed a couple of white things blowing in the wind. Taking a closer look, the napkins that had been under the cover of the calendar book at the top of the stack of books I had left on top of the car were fluttering away. Putting the car back into park, I got out to get the books and what I saw was startling! The cover of the calendar book that was now open had opened against the wind, and it was still open, while the thinner pages had not been moved.

Could this have been one of those simple coincidences, or was it the breath of God moving a book cover against the wind, releasing the napkins to get my attention, so I would not lose my Bible, schoolwork, address/phone book, and calendar/appointment book? I was instantly reminded of the line that I had written just minutes earlier: *The longer that I trust Jesus, the more I realize the many places that He intercedes for me and protects me from harm.* I was overwhelmed by this simple act of love from God.

In years gone by, I would have never recognized what had just happened, any more than I understood the meaning of Proverbs 3:5–6: *Trust in the LORD with all thine heart; and lean not unto thine own understanding. In all thy ways acknowledge him, and he shall direct thy paths.*

Larry, my good friend for many years, interpreted this for me, breaking the verses down to something I can understand. Larry said God takes care of those who are too ignorant to take care of themselves. I know that he is correct.

CHAPTER 22

False Religion
That Entertains Sin

After traveling much of the night in the mountains of Arkansas, it was about breakfast time, but there were not many places to eat. I prefer to get out of the van and at least walk into a place for food. The little walk from the vehicle to the counter inside may not seem like much, but after sitting and driving for several hours, it is refreshing to stand up and do a little walking. This morning, in this sparsely populated part of the country, I felt it would be good to find anything open at all. While coming to a wide spot in the road that has a very large and busy sawmill, there was a Sonic Drive-In. There wasn't much of anything else in the little town besides a gas station. Sonic is not usually my first choice for a breakfast place, but it beats having no breakfast by quite a bit, so that was my choice. Perhaps over time I have become spoiled by the dollar menu and senior coffee at Mickey D's. After enjoying a breakfast wrap of sorts, I continued driving south, now mostly out of the beautiful mountains, and entered the rolling flatland. I came upon a young man walking along the side of the road who was dressed in work clothes, with no luggage or anything else with him, so I stopped and offered him a ride.

He told me that he was a mechanic at the sawmill/lumber company I had just passed, and because the company had nothing for him to do that day, they were sending him home. He further told me that he was twenty-two, had graduated from high school and mechanical trade school, had a job, was a Christian, had a pickup truck that was in the shop for repairs, and lived close to his parents and grandparents in the next community. He also told me that he had a girlfriend he had met in high school, and they had been together for several years. In asking him what he meant by them being together, he told me that they lived together and had a child together. In asking him why they were not married, he said that he was willing, but she was not, because she was just not sure that she was ready. "What do you mean, not sure?" I asked in complete surprise. Without getting a response from him to that question, I asked whether he knew the song, "Oh How I Love Jesus." As I began to sing the first verse, he began singing it with me.

There is a name I love to hear, I love to sing its worth;

It sounds like music in my ear, the sweetest name on earth.

Oh, how I love Jesus, Oh, how I love Jesus, Oh, how I love Jesus,

Because He first loved me.

I stopped singing and asked him if he really meant what he was singing, being a believer in Jesus Christ himself, and he assured me that he did. Then I asked him what he supposed Jesus might have meant when He said in John 14:15: *If ye love me, keep my commandments.* He told me that meant we were to obey the commandments. Then I asked him which commandments were we to obey, and he answered, "The Ten Commandments." I then inquired what he thought the seventh commandment, *Thou shalt not commit adultery*, meant. He very accurately explained what it meant.

The beauty of giving strangers a ride is that they will listen as long as they want to ride, and almost always they have a need in their life that is not being ministered to. I look at these times as divine appointments and thank the Lord for each one of them and His giving me the opportunity to share His love and guidance. Without a doubt, this young man was one of those appointments, and he even told me that he thought the Lord had sent me along.

We had almost come to where he lived, so when I kindly but firmly said to him, "You seem to be an intelligent young man in that you finished school, and with purpose in your life chose an honorable vocation. You are willing to work to meet your responsibilities and are active in going to church, and love your family. I have no doubt that you love the Lord and want to do what is right regarding Him, so why are you not doing that?" Without giving him time to respond, I continued by saying that he looked like a healthy, handsome, and smart man, the kind of guy a lady would want for a husband. That was God's plan. God even performed the first wedding, joining Adam and Eve together as husband and wife. God knew that man would need a companion, a helpmeet, a wife. I reminded him that he had found a girl he liked well enough to live with and have children with, and challenged him to immediately tell her that he was the marrying kind, to tell her that he would like to obey the Lord who saved him, and that he did not want to commit adultery any longer. If she would not marry him, then they would just have to quit playing house, so he could then perhaps find a woman who would want to be his wife.

By then, we were in front of his house. Clearly, he wasn't in any hurry to get out, so we continued talking for a few minutes, as I encouraged him to live for the Lord, and be a good testimony to those he worked with who did not know Christ as their Savior. Why would they want the kind of religion he had when he was blatantly living in adultery?

He thanked me several times for telling him the truth about his relationship with Jesus, and encouraging him to be a man of God, truly living for the Lord. Whether he followed through and changed the course of his life, I probably will not know this side of heaven, but I pray that he takes advantage of the encouragement to get right with the Lord, the mother of his child, his parents and grandparents, and that he becomes a strong part of the Lord's work at the local church.

There are many others who have this same perverted religion that they have invented, trusting their own pernicious ways instead of the commands of the Lord they claim to love. I am reminded of what Scripture says:

> *This know also, that in the last days perilous times shall come. For men shall be lovers of their own selves, covetous, boasters, proud, blasphemers, disobedient to parents, unthankful, unholy, Without natural affection, trucebreakers, false accusers, incontinent, fierce, despisers of those that are good, Traitors, heady, high-minded, lovers of pleasures more than lovers of God; Having a form of godliness, but denying the power thereof: from such turn away. For of this sort are they which creep into houses, and lead captive silly women laden with sins, led away with divers lusts, Ever learning, and never able to come to the knowledge of the truth* (2 Timothy 3:1–7).

> *But the fearful, and unbelieving, and the abominable, and murderers, and whoremongers, and sorcerers, and idolaters, and all liars, shall have their part in the lake which burneth with fire and brimstone: which is the second death* (Revelation 21:8).

CHAPTER 23

Visits With My Sister Nancy Jo Nance

I thank God for the gift of a loving, caring friend, the only blood sister I will ever have. With her being two and a half years older than me, the last of the litter, she kind of thought of herself as my great protector, instructor, adviser, and provider.

Her final battle with cancer ended December 13, 2011, when she went on to be with the Lord. She had accepted Jesus as her only hope of heaven over thirty years ago, and believed His promise to her, as I do: *My sheep hear my voice, and I know them, and they follow me: And I give unto them eternal life; and they shall never perish, neither shall any man pluck them out of my hand. My Father, which gave them me, is greater than all; and no man is able to pluck them out of my Father's hand. I and my Father are one* (John 10:27–30).

Among the earliest visits with my sister that come to mind was the day she took me to school with her. She must have been in the first grade, because her reading book was *Dick and Jane*, and they were learning the words. It seemed to me that Nancy was the smartest and prettiest girl in the class, and I was proud to be her little brother. I was completely fascinated by the thought that I too could learn to read and go on adventures wherever I was just by learning what the words in a book meant. She soon taught me to read that entire book. I could hardly wait until I too could go to school and learn the wonderful things that she knew.

Things did not always go as they should. Several years passed, and we moved to Mississippi, to a small religious community where we worked together on a farm and in a hospital/rest home. We did practically everything together, but each family had their own house. After another few years, we moved back to Kansas. She was now in high school and driving our parents' car. The only problem was that she had to take me with her when she took the car. I believe the intention was that she wouldn't do anything she shouldn't do while I was along. About all I can say about that is that for a very small price my lips were sealed, until one day we were caught in the very act of deceit by our dad. That seemed to be the end of that era.

I had finally reached that day when I was to graduate from junior high school. They were having a big-deal graduation, where everyone would walk across the stage and receive their diploma. Our parents both worked and didn't have a lot, even though I have learned that they were rich in the things that really count – family and their relationship with the Lord – but they would have been unable to buy new, fancy clothing for me to wear at the graduation. Nancy also had a job, and decided that I should wear a new suit to the graduation, so she bought me a complete suit, including new shoes for the ceremony. I went from being a boy who didn't think very well of himself to a young man with a little confidence that day when I received a certificate of completion for that level of my education. I was also the best-dressed person who walked across the stage, all made possible by a loving, caring, giving sister. If I seem at times to be a little over-confident, it began that day under my sister's tutelage.

Shortly after my graduation, Nancy got married and began to have a family. A few years later I joined the Navy. Both of our lives seemed to take a few turns for the worse, otherwise known as surrendering to sin. When we were together, which was not often, we would be up almost all night talking about what we were into, and perhaps gaining confidence in our pernicious ways, knowing that one was no worse than the other, thereby justifying ourselves. There was nothing hidden between us, and we were never shocked by what the other one said. I do not believe that there is another person on earth who ever knew the real Earl as my sister Nance did, and I doubt there is any other that she was so completely open with.

After being honorably discharged from the Navy, I met and married Rebecca, and Nancy became as her loving "mother-in-law." Our mother had died a few years earlier, but even if she had not, Nancy would still have treated Rebecca the same. A few years after we were married, I came to the realization that if I died, I would have no hope of heaven, because of my sinfulness, and that scared me very much. In our religious upbringing, we were taught of heaven and hell, God, Jesus, and the devil, and that sinners went to hell with the devil, while non-sinners went to heaven. There was so much evidence in my life that I was a sinner that I had to find a cure for that. A good friend told me that the only cure for my condition was to accept what Jesus had already done for me.

I confessed my belief in Jesus, accepting the gift of eternal life that was mine through Him, and I have never been the same since.

After this, the visits I had with Nancy were different. Yes, we would still talk almost all night about things when we were together, but it was totally different. She also came to a saving knowledge of Jesus Christ somewhere around that time. We would talk of what we thought heaven would be like and who would be there, realizing that not all good people would be there, just those who accepted Jesus' gift of life in Him. We talked about what we might be able to do to convince our loved ones and all others of their need for Jesus. We've experienced quite a few victories for Jesus, but there are many who have not accepted Him. I pray that they will before it is eternally too late.

The next time that I will see my dear sister Nancy will be in heaven, where we can forever rejoice because of the love and mercy of Jesus our Christ, and where there will be no more pain or death. I, for one, am looking forward to that great eternal day.

CHAPTER 24

Result of a Bone-Chilling Wind in Chicago

Coming from the car with a bag of Gospel of John and Romans booklets to give to anyone who wanted one, I began to realize just how cold and cutting the wind was while crossing the parking lot at Pacific Garden Mission in Chicago. Somehow it came to my mind that if you think you are in misery (not to be mistaken for Missouri), consider how Jesus must have felt that day He was hanging on the cruel cross of Calvary because of you! Talk about getting someone's attention; He certainly had mine now.

I am thankful that I am allowed to speak to the guests at Pacific Garden Mission several times each month as I go to the places where the Lord has opened doors for me to preach the gospel of salvation in and through Jesus, to a great collection of homeless people. Many of these people are looking for answers that will give them a hope for the future during the rest of their lives. There is a multitude of reasons why the guests are there, but the common theme is that something has not worked or has gone terribly wrong in their lives, leaving them with little of substance and in a vacuum of hopelessness. This was one of those occasions. I had the privilege of speaking at the noon chapel service, seeing several people make decisions for Christ, and now it was about time for the men's five o'clock Bible study, and I needed some supplies from the car.

Having encountered the chill of Chicago's cold north winter wind, and being reminded that my temporary discomfort was absolutely nothing as compared to the suffering that Jesus had allowed Himself to be subjected to because of my sinfulness, there could be no better subject for the Bible study than what Jesus had done for all of us on Calvary's cross. Even though there are usually some topics in my mind about what to speak on, more often than not I am not exactly sure what the topic will be until the last minute before it is time to speak, and this was one of those times.

Well over twenty years ago, as a relatively new man serving under Dr. Parker Dailey in the ministry at Blue Ridge Baptist Temple in Kansas City, Missouri, one of my duties was the ministry of tape production. One Sunday night, we had a very well-known man of God, Dr. David Cavin, who would soon be speaking, so I asked him what the title of his message and Scripture text was to be. I was quite surprised when his response was that he did not know. He then told me that the Holy Spirit had not given it to him yet, and sometimes he did not know what the topic and text would be until he was standing behind the pulpit. I do not remember what his sermon was, but I do remember the delivery being superb and pointed, and a message that challenged many with the truth. I thought at the time that to be in tune to the leading of the Holy Spirit to that degree would be a great blessing to a minister. The Spirit knows the needs of the people much better that any man could.

The Lord has led me to that type of ministry, relying on the Holy Spirit to lead me each time. This kind of speaking, however, cannot be done without careful preparation. One must read, study, and remember God's Word, and communicate often with the Lord in prayer and meditation, seeking His face and His direction. Scripture even tells me that this is the Lord's will: *Trust in the LORD with all thine heart; and lean not unto thine own understanding. In all thy ways acknowledge him, and he shall direct thy paths* (Proverbs 3:5–6). It must be noted that the Holy Spirit can give a man of God this information well in advance or at the time of delivery. Not knowing what the message will be in advance really works on my prayer life and helps me depend wholly on the Lord.

On this occasion, the sudden thought of preaching about the misery of Jesus Christ on the cross and why He submitted Himself to this torture was a frightful thought because of the very serious nature of the subject. It requires telling people of His love for fallen sinners, which includes us all, as well as giving a clear presentation of what we must do to receive the gift of salvation personally. The portion of Scripture that I used was John 18:28–19:30, which begins with Jesus being delivered to the cowardly Pilate to be crucified. He was taken there by the religious leaders of that day, because their power was being eroded by the simple truth of His message, and they had to take desperate measures to maintain their status. Even though Pilate said at least three times that he found no fault in Jesus, he had him scourged and whipped to within inches of killing him, and let his soldiers abuse Jesus in many ways, by pulling out His beard, driving a wreath of thorns into His skull, and slapping, beating, and spitting on Him. Jesus then carried the cross to the place of His execution, where His hands and feet were nailed to it, and it was put into a hole in the ground so it would stand up. Jesus hung there naked, being mocked by them until He died. Thankfully that is not the end of the story. That is what Jesus did for us sinners, paying for our sins with His own blood. Sin always requires a blood sacrifice, so Jesus paid our sin debt with His blood, and if we accept that gift, we will have eternal life with Him according to John 3:16–18, Romans 10:9–13, and John 10:28–30.

This message was lovingly delivered to these men, and I invited them to receive this gift of salvation from Jesus. It makes me thankful to the Lord for sending that cold blast of Chicago wind to remind me of the very heart of our hope of salvation – the misery that Jesus experienced – so that we could have life everlasting. The sad part is that not everyone will receive Him, but as many as do, they go instantly from everlasting damnation to everlasting life in Jesus.

Song Service

There was seemingly the potential for an enjoyable and uplifting song service as people came into the chapel area visiting with each other. They appeared to be ready for the service, or at least willing to start, so we could get it over with. We had just finished a filling and tasty hot meal and were seated in a comfortable and quiet room suitable for a little nap, if the preacher didn't get too loud.

Attending chapel service is mandatory at this mission, and the service should last about one hour. Sometimes it is hard to get it all finished in that short of a time, but anything said after that hour is over except "You are dismissed" will not be received very well, if heard at all.

Not wanting to kid myself, I realized that the only reason most of them were there was because if they wanted to enjoy the food and shelter, this also must be endured. If I think about it, it makes me feel really special. Being reminded that this is not a popularity contest, and that it is not about me, I try to remain flexible, trying to be prepared to continue through any distraction, so the service will not be interrupted. Sometimes I must remind myself that thirty-seven years ago I too was just a practicing heathen without Jesus, who was very good at being lost. So why should I expect some of the lost people here to act any differently than I did?

The people were now assembled in the chapel. The night mission staff person had finished roll call, and I was introduced. Prayer was given, and now it was my turn to do what I love to do: attempt to get and keep their attention, while telling them how much Jesus loves them and that He wants a relationship with them. Almost always I follow the same pattern learned from attending church for many years, beginning with prayer and singing, followed by the message, and ending with an evangelistic invitation, inviting people to decide for Jesus Christ without delay. This evening was not going to be any exception.

I try to involve the mission guests by letting them have input in the service. They are asked to find a song they would like for us to sing together, and then let me know which one it is by lifting their hand to be recognized, and then telling me which one it is. This works best when we use the *Sparrow Ministry* "Songs to Live By" songbook, where we have only fourteen songs to choose from. Surprising as it may seem, I happen to know them all. This evening we were using their songbooks, which included some songs I have never heard, and without a pianist, we are somewhat limited in what we can sing together. As sometimes happens, the first request this evening was a number blurted out by a young man with one of those "got-you" grins on his face. After turning to the page and seeing that I had never heard this song, I asked if anyone knew it. No one did, including or especially me. I then asked the young man if he could sing just a little of it and maybe I could pick it up. He then admitted that he just said a number to see what we would do. As it turned out, he was the one embarrassed, so we went on and sang another song that everyone did know, and it went very well.

The next song selected was a well-known song, and most everyone was singing well, except that it sounded like we were singing in rounds. It was not "Row, Row, Row Your Boat," that song we sang at camp or while traveling. My parents probably would have liked to have a radio to listen to, but all they had were three boys and a girl. We were always singing. I'm not sure that it was a "joyful noise," but at least it was loud, especially when we were trying to sing in rounds, with each trying to be heard over the other.

Getting back to the song we were singing, a new distraction had developed. A man who was probably in his forties was amusing himself and attempting to amuse others by waving his hands, as though he was leading the music. Perhaps this was inspired by the lack of some people using the same timing as the others. At the end of the song I told the people, "There is a man who is trying to learn how to lead singing and he is getting better at it. As soon as he gets it right, I may ask him to help lead the singing." He kind of slid down in his seat and put his hands down. It always amazes me how when I yield to their desire for personal attention, they usually are not so willing to have it. I decided it was just another attempt the deceiver was making to try to keep people from hearing the words of the song that could cause them to give some attention to Jesus.

The next song caused the one person who had a good and loud voice, and who was always about a half a word behind all the others, to sing even louder. I asked that we all try to sing together, but that was not to be. As pastor of a church that did not have a song leader, I believe the Lord was preparing me for such a time as this. We had a mentally challenged man in his late twenties who loved to sing loud, but he could not read, so as soon as he heard what you were singing, he would copy it, causing somewhat of the round effect. In noticing that this man at the mission was not using a songbook, it was apparent that he was doing the same thing. Even though there was nothing I could do to correct the problem, short of not singing any more songs, it was the perfect time and place to park the songbooks.

At this particular mission, the guests included men, women, and children. The men are separated from the women and children by a couple of taped-off empty rows, and this arrangement worked well, keeping that potential distraction at a minimum. But sometimes the little children do not find my speaking very interesting or entertaining, and they are brutally honest in letting everyone know with their cries of torment and anguish. One such child was in attendance that evening, and he was loudly protesting being there. I tried to assure the mother that it was not bothering me, but to tell you the truth, I believe the mother thought I was bothering the child, because she took the child out and did not return.

We had survived the attempt to be distracted to the point of being pulled away from completing the message of salvation. The devil did not get the victory that he was trying so hard to get. Out of the approximately thirty people who were in attendance, there was a young lady, around twenty years old, who had raised her hand requesting prayer, so she could know that when she died or Jesus came back again, she would be with Him. I led in prayer, inviting people to pray with me if they were serious about wanting a saving relationship with Jesus and about asking Him also to be the Lord of their lives. After the prayer, she stood in testimony, asking Jesus to be her Savior. Her face radiated with the joy that Jesus gives to those who will come to Him, proving that no matter what the distractions are, the Lord can still work in changing people's hearts.

The Bible clearly tells us: *For whosoever shall call upon the name of the Lord shall be saved* (Romans 10:13).

CHAPTER 26

Passing of a Godly Mother

While traveling to speak at Denver Rescue Mission in Denver, Colorado, I encountered one of those divine appointments that I so look forward to and try to be aware of when they happen. They are one of the rewarding parts of this excellent adventure of being a traveling missionary evangelist.

It worked well for me to leave Trenton, Missouri, the evening before I was to speak in Denver, because after a couple of rest stops, it left plenty of time to enjoy the day without being rushed. Part of that enjoyment came by stopping at the big Golden Arches for a wonderful bowl of fluffy oats with diced apples and raisins to begin the day with.

I suppose one reason that food is so appealing to me stems from the admiration I had for the big, beautiful, strong horses that my dad worked with at a farm in Mississippi, down near Chunky, a town of perhaps one hundred people, when I was around seven years old. The horses were given a big tin can of grain, perhaps oats, sometimes with a little molasses on top, before they were taken to the field to pull the plow or whatever work they had to do. Because that worked for them, it may also work for me. I have heard the statement, "strong as a horse," as well as "dumb as an ox," and if I were to choose to be like one or the other, even though they both like oats, I would choose the horse, even though others may have other ideas regarding me.

Back to western Kansas. While I was seated at the Arches, where I was able to keep an eye on the *sparrowmobile,* and while munching away on the oats, I couldn't help but hear two men having a conversation. They were seated at a booth directly behind me. One of them began talking about his mother. The story was a compelling one. What really got my attention was when he was telling of her faith in God, the Christian influence she had on others, and her long, full life with children and grandchildren. She had outlived his dad and advanced to the need of support at a retirement home. She had been taken to a hospital where her life on earth had ended. Her son, who was probably in his seventies, was telling the story.

The staff at the hospital called to inform him that the prospects of his mother, who was over ninety years old, did not appear to be very promising, and he should come to the hospital. As I recall, he said that when he got there and went into her room, she seemed to be in a coma or asleep and was having difficulty breathing. He said that he then took off his shoes and glasses and got into the bed beside her. While lying beside her, she responded to his presence by waking up. They talked a little, then sang some beloved hymns and shared a time of prayer. She then laid her head on his shoulder as she breathed her last, and peacefully her soul and spirit went to be with the Lord, in whom she had trusted for eternal salvation as a young person.

Her funeral must have been preplanned, because he said that two of the chosen pallbearers could not be immediately located at first, but somehow were contacted in time for them to serve. The lady who had always fixed her hair was also able to come and fix it for her one last time, and her son said that she looked twenty years younger and so much at peace for the service. Included in the plans was a woman whose singing she had enjoyed and who had agreed to sing at this eventuality, but now that the time was here, she was very heavy with child, and delivered a healthy baby the day before the funeral. Surprisingly, she was able to sing all the requested songs in a good voice. The son told the other man that to begin with it seemed all the plans were going wrong, but it all came together just as his mother had wanted, and it was a beautiful celebration of her life.

He had so many words of praise for his godly mother and her faith in Jesus, which he had also accepted. He told of how they enjoyed worshiping the Lord together over the years, and on many occasions had lifted their voices together in songs of praise and worship of the Savior.

Hearing this heartwarming story brought to my mind the passing of my own godly mother. That story is very different from the story just told. She was a godly woman with a son named Earl who had no hope of a future with Jesus. Thanks to the mercy of God, that part changed in my life. When I was about thirty, some twelve years after my mother went to be with the Lord, I accepted the gift of eternal salvation in Jesus by confessing with my mouth my belief that Jesus did die for sinners such as me, and believing in my heart that God raised Him from the dead. That is the hope of my salvation, which will result in being with my mother and most of the rest of my family, along with the multitudes of believers in Jesus, for all eternity. How much sweeter the passing of my mother and dad would have been had I given my heart to Jesus sooner.

There is nothing any of us can do to reclaim lost time or change our past, but we can humble ourselves before Jesus, confessing our belief in His payment for our wrongdoings on Calvary's cross in presenting Himself as our only hope of heaven. This will radically redirect our future, moving us from eternal damnation to hell with the devil and his followers, to an eternity in heaven with Jesus and His followers. Praise be to God. Think about it! Are YOU personally ready for this eventuality? I spoke to the man in this story for permission to write and publish this, and he verbally gave me that permission. My prayer is that God will be honored by their actions as well as by mine.

Learning a Lesson about Trusting God

We, the Nance family, had moved to northern Missouri from Kansas City, so I could serve as senior pastor at a relatively new church at Chillicothe. (It is easy to remember how to spell it by using the tune in the "Mickey Mouse" song.)

After living in Kansas City for almost twenty years with all kinds of shopping and other activities available to us almost around the clock, and being on the pastoral staff of a church that averaged well over one thousand in attendance every Sunday, we moved to a town of less than seven thousand people and a church with an average attendance of less than twenty people, a farm town that had just come through the big farm crunch. It was no surprise to me that the Mickey Mouse tune came to my mind.

Dr. Parker Dailey, my pastor in Kansas City, told me that this would be a real challenge. If the church grew and was successful, that would be great, but if it did not, I should remember that several other men had given it their best, without any great victory stories to tell, so if it did not work for me, at least I could say that I had experience in pastoral ministry. As usual, he knew exactly what he was talking about. It was an experience I shall never forget. It wasn't all good, and it wasn't all bad, but at times it peaked past the limit of both extremes. There were plenty of ministry opportunities, and we were witnessing some victories, which resulted in minimal growth, but growing even faster was our financial disaster.

While in Kansas City, Rebecca and I both had good-paying jobs, two house payments, and other debt that was very manageable, but upon moving to Chillicothe, we left behind our sources of income without leaving behind our debt. The new church promised me twenty dollars a week, whether I needed it or not, and a tremendous challenge. We were helped for a short time by some sister churches in Missouri, but that was short-lived, and the grim reality began to set in that if we were without the God that we trusted in, we were on our own. There were many times when I wondered if I had made a horrible mistake, but there was no turning back.

Being the trooper that she has always been, Rebecca found employment in a neighboring town at considerably lower wages than she had in Kansas City. As our support from the other churches began to dwindle, I began to scramble, trying to find meaningful part-time employment outside of the church. Not being willing to make a job outside of the church my first priority, it became difficult, but I had to remind myself constantly why we now lived where we did and that the Lord would never leave or forsake us.

Finally there was an opening as a school bus driver, so I applied for it and was hired, which helped arrest the downward spiral some, but we were still slipping behind. To supplement our income further, I began building a few wood products that we sold at craft stores and outdoor festivals, as well as doing some mechanical repairs on small equipment. Our daughter Angela was now a senior and was only required to attend school until noon, and then she would come to our shop and help make and sell wood crafts.

We generally had lunch together before we got into the projects of the day. One day when she came to work, it was clear that something was really troubling her. She then told me that there was a bright orange notice hanging on the front door of our house that said our electricity would be shut off at three o'clock that very afternoon if we did not pay some five hundred dollars-plus by that given time. She really wanted to know what we were going to do. Fact is, I didn't know what to do. I only had five dollars in cash and nothing in the bank or anywhere else. We were broke, and in a few hours we would probably be in the dark. We were both surprised at what I said next, with a calm assurance that made it seem everything would be okay. (Really? How can that be? What was going through my mind? I needed to remain calm so as not to make matters worse.) Then, I took the five dollars out of my pocket, gave it to Angie, and told her to go to the little corner grill and get us our usual – two brown-bag specials – which included two cheeseburgers, two orders of fries, and a medium drink. This being all the money we had, we both wondered if this was the correct thing to do, but that small amount of money would not solve our much greater problem, so that is what we did.

When she returned with our lunch, we sat at the table, asked the Lord to bless it and somehow see us through our other problems, and give me wisdom to do whatever He would have me do. For whatever reason lunch was especially tasty and satisfying as we discussed different possibilities for lights at home. I suggested that we copy from the many Amish people we lived around. There was a big box of candles I had bought at an auction, and this looked like a perfect time to begin using them. Neither one of us was very delighted at the prospect, but we were out of options, and if the Amish could do it, why couldn't

FLIGHT OF THE SPARROW

we? We dropped that subject because we did not have another plan, and it didn't seem that there was anything else we could do. Now that lunch was over and it was time to go to our separate projects at our shop, I was impressed to ask Angie to go back to the house and check the mailbox. I was not expecting anything to be in it, but felt compelled to look there.

She went to the house and soon returned with an envelope in her hand. It didn't seem to have anything in it, but upon opening it, there was a check. The amount of the check was equal to the utility bill, two brown-bag lunches, and a few extra dollars. There was no written explanation. We were both convinced that the Lord had heard our prayer and had already sent the answer to it in advance. It was a lesson that I may never have learned had I stayed at the place of security in Kansas City. Rebecca, Angie, and Mike were all there with me to live it, and our lives were changed and enriched because of it. Why should I ever doubt that the Lord will meet the needs of His workers? He has never let me down. This was a turning point for me in the ministry. It was not the end of all problems, but now I knew the solution for all of them, and His name was Jesus the Christ.

A dear friend of ours who didn't know of our desperate situation had received a bonus from his employer, and the Lord laid it on his heart to share a portion of it with us. I pray that the Lord will continue to bless him and his family.

CHAPTER 28

Trust Jesus in All Things

Snow was falling and the wind was blowing as I was leaving Chicago (no wonder they call it the Windy City), on February 12, 2010. I had spoken to an accumulation of hundreds of people after speaking six times in the last twenty-six hours. Now, being very tired, I was not looking forward to this normal eight-hour trip, and was trying to just wish myself home. Even a much-dedicated dreamer cannot make that happen, and I knew just what it would take to make the trip but was running low on that ingredient: endurance. As before, it was just a matter of getting in the car, buckling myself in (there are a lot of crazies out there; perhaps one is even in my car), starting the car, putting it in gear, pressing the gas pedal, and going. The desire to be home after a few days on the road motivated me to get in the car and just get the trip over with.

Leaving Chicago, traveling south on I-55, the first fifty miles went very slowly because of the snow, a few fender benders, and wet, messy roads. The temperature was hovering around freezing, but because the roads had been treated, praise the Lord, they were not icy. If everything went well, I didn't expect to be home much before midnight. Even though traffic remained somewhat heavy on that Friday evening, the snow, for the most part, had let up, leaving me with wet and salty roads, and a dirty windshield. Truck traffic is always very heavy on that interstate, leaving me to wonder whether all the roads leading into Chicago are that packed with trucks, and what do they do with all that stuff?

As I was progressing south on the two hundred miles to Springfield, Illinois, the prospect of an improvement in weather continued, but the other potential problem seemed to be nagging away from time to time. The *sparrowmobile* seemed to lose some power once in a while, then straighten out and run right. Before I arrived in Springfield, where I was to turn east, it became increasingly apparent that the motor was getting weaker, so I stopped in Springfield at Wally World, had supper, went for a walk (to satisfy the doctor's plea for my health), and bought some fuel additive (HEAT) for the car. Rebecca was away from home in central Missouri staying with our granddaughters while our daughter was away on business, so I had no real urgent reason to get home. As I stepped out of the store to return to my car, I found that there had been a radical change in the weather.

Snow was now coming down very fast, and part of the time it seemed to be snowing horizontally. The temperature was also rapidly taking a frigid plunge. The continued trip west had no promise of being pleasant. Before leaving Springfield and because of the snow, I topped off the gas tank, added the HEAT, and prayed for traveling mercy. Now heading west on US 36 in the blinding snow for the final two hundred and fifty miles of this journey, I chose to fall in behind a truck that was traveling at what I believed to be an appropriate speed. It was necessary to keep up with it, because at anything more than approximately ten car lengths behind it, it began to disappear in the blinding snow.

After a while I began thinking of that really tall bridge that crosses over the Illinois River, with two lanes going in each direction on the twin bridges. It seemed to me that the side barriers were not high enough and way, way too close together in good conditions, not to mention this current situation of snow-covered roads, and the hill that you had to climb while traveling west. The only way that I could continue progressing toward home was to put my nagging fears aside, trust completely in the Lord to be with me, and then carefully continue on. I was thinking that I would rather have crossed an old-fashioned covered bridge, the kind they built for horses that were afraid of heights. At least I could reason with myself that at the very least I had some horse sense.

By the mercy of God it had quit snowing before I came to that dreaded river crossing, so my only worry would be the potential for ice on a wet bridge (what a comforting thought). Generally, I don't try to drive in the very middle of a two-lane road, but that is where I found myself that night, since there was no other traffic in sight. Perhaps the other people had a little more than "horse sense" and had either gotten off the road or just stayed home. I made it across the bridge without incident, and eventually arrived at the Mississippi River bridge (a much safer-looking bridge), and was cruising toward home with about one hundred and fifty miles to go. If all continued to go well, I should be home no later than 1:30 a.m. Saturday. That would be plenty of time to rest before traveling to speak in Topeka, Kansas, that night.

Driving along into the cold and windy night, and still around seventy miles from home, the van began to lose power and was overheating, so I pulled over and stopped to check the coolant, which was fine, and the temperature returned to normal. I then proceeded on toward home. After a few more miles, it seemed like the cruise control had kicked off, and at the same time a cloud of steam came from under the hood. The wind was really blowing, so with all the road noise, I didn't at first realize that the engine had stopped turning. At this point, I coasted as far to the side as I could without leaving the paved shoulder. I did not want to be stuck in the mud along with whatever this new problem was. With a hot engine, the first thing I needed to do was to let it cool off. That should not take too long, because by now it was around ten degrees, and the wind was still blowing strongly.

While waiting in the darkness and watching for the occasional car coming along so I could turn on the hazard lights to warn them of my position, I decided that it would be a great time to pray, letting God know about His broken car, and asking Him what He was going to do about it. Isn't it great to be able to give everything to God, especially when it is not working? Fifteen or twenty minutes had now passed, and I was still waiting for an answer, which did not seem to be coming. Since the engine had cooled enough to check it out, I again checked the coolant, and it was not low enough to cause the problems I now had, and the oil level was fine. It was time to try to restart the engine. It turned over more freely than it should have, and two of the six cylinders seemed to fire on each revolution. There was only one thing I knew of that could cause all of these symptoms, and that was that the camshaft must not be turning. The engine cannot run without that, and it being a major repair, the van was not going anywhere under its own power.

It was now time to see whom God would send to rescue me. Calling 9-1-1, I told them of the traffic hazard caused by my vehicle being on the shoulder of the road, and could they send some help. A few minutes later a sheriff arrived, and while heading to his car with him, I called a couple of numbers that he provided, but at midnight on this cold windy night, no one answered the phone. Upon calling back in, the sheriff was given yet one more number. Praise God that this man answered his phone and was soon out hooking up God's van to his tow truck. This total breakdown happened just seventeen miles from Freedom Baptist Church, pastored by Ron Adrian, just outside of Brookfield. The pastor and the church are friends and active partners of the *Sparrow Ministry* with their prayers and gifts, so I asked the tow truck driver to take the van there, and we would put it in the corner of their parking lot. On the way there, I learned that he was an active member of another local sister church, and we discussed why I happened to be out in the cold. When we were just about to the church, I told him that if the tow bill was under a certain amount, I could pay him cash, pay with a card, write a check, or promise him that the check would be in the mail. He never responded to or commented on any of those offers. We pulled up to the parking place, and he began to unhook the van. About that time someone came out of the dark church building to see what was going on. The tow truck driver was starting to leave, and I asked him what I owed. He told me that this would be a contribution to this ministry. What a blessing people are who love the Lord and are called according to His purpose.

Back to the man at the church. In the darkness, I could not see who it was, so I walked up to him and saw that it was the youth leader of the church. Would you believe that they were having an overnight sleepover for the teens, and the church was warm, so he welcomed me in. After thinking about it for a millisecond, considering my other choice of staying in a cold car until morning, I accepted the invitation. The youth group left early that morning, leaving me to my own devices. With Rebecca out of town, I could not call her to rescue me, and if anyone else were to take me to Trenton, I would be stuck without a car, so a rental car seemed to be the answer. Looking in the phone book, there was only one car rental place in the area, and as it happened, it was less than one mile from the church. They would come pick me up and yes, they had one car available.

The car worked out fine, and things went well in Topeka that night, with many making decisions for Jesus. I spent most of the next week trying to find a suitable vehicle, but everything I thought I could use was impossible for me to purchase. In desperation, I returned to the Ford dealer in Trenton and was able to purchase a much better car than I would have ever chosen. It is working well, and God is more than able to keep it on the road. It was like getting out of a rowboat and boarding a cabin cruiser. It is my opinion that everything in this story was a divine appointment and was planned by God. His ways and plans are so much better than mine, and I love being His messenger.

CHAPTER 29

You Decide

A gain I found myself at one of my favorite places in East Texas, spending some quality time at the Golden Arches, home of senior coffee, the dollar menu, air conditioning, computer power outlets, as well as free wireless Internet access, and last but by all means not least, clean restrooms. You decide! If you had twenty-three hours to make the three-hour drive between Shreveport, Louisiana, and Dallas, Texas, and it was over eighty degrees out, not to mention the frequent source of excellent adventures that result in *Flight of the Sparrow* stories, wouldn't you stop also? Stopping this day did not leave me empty or disappointed.

I arrived in the parking lot around 11:00 a.m. I was there less than five minutes when a well-groomed, healthy-looking man, perhaps in his late thirties, wearing worn blue jeans and a stained T-shirt, came up to the side of the car, leaned down, and indicated a desire to speak with me. So I rolled the window down to hear what he wanted. Immediately he dropped to one knee so we were able to speak face to face.

He began by telling me that he had made a bad mistake. I expected him to confess to wasting his substance on riotous living, but that was not the mistake he wanted to confess. Instead, he continued by telling me that he had come to this part of Texas from Houston because he had found a job, but the job didn't pan out, so now he was trying to raise money for fuel for his relatively new pickup truck to return home. He told me that he had never done this sort of thing before (asking for money from a stranger), but now, in his desperation, he was willing to work, wash my car, sell me his tools, or do anything else that he could for money. This caused me to wonder what kind of work did he suppose that I, clearly a traveler with out-of-state license plates, have for him to do? Or where might he wash my clean car? Or why would a worker be so willing to sell his tools? Or just what exactly would he be willing to do for money? What would you make of all this? You decide if you will!

At that point, he put his hand behind him and whipped out a large four-by-six-inch glossy color photo of a woman about his age holding a cute little toddler. Interestingly enough, the photo was not wrinkled and had no fold marks, and was not soiled in any way. It looked like a new photo, not something that one would expect to see a traveling man produce. This new photo evidence, or prop, presented more questions than it had answers to offer. You decide: Was it actually a photo of his family, or a cunningly devised sales pitch?

I told the man that I was not sure I would be able to help him, but I knew of a rescue mission in Longview, Texas, the Highway 80 Rescue Mission, which provided food, shelter, and direction for people in need, and they would probably be glad to help him. I then asked him if he had any church affiliation. To this question he cheerfully responded, "I am an active member of First Baptist of Houston, a Southern Baptist Church." With this new information, I felt more committed to helping him, a brother in Christ. Next, I told him that because of his involvement in the Lord's work, we could contact his pastor, or another leader in the church, and I would extend to him whatever help that they deemed he needed and were willing to cover financially. Instead of telling me his pastor's name or the church phone number, however, he said that he would go to his truck and make a few calls.

While he was in his truck, Mike, our ministry assistant, and I were discussing who this man could be calling. Could it be his pastor, or just someone pretending to be, or was he attempting to devise a larger scam?

There was another fact I did not intend to omit, and I am not sure at what point in our conversation I had told him about my being in this parking lot two months before, and that I was approached by a man with a similar story. He too had a picture of a child on his cell phone and he had clearly, without question, scammed me out of twenty dollars, and because of the number of panhandlers in this area, they were teaching me that not everyone was honest. With a shocked look on his face, he assured me that he was not one of them. For some reason, though, he seemed to know exactly what I was talking about. Please help me decide. Was he an innocent traveler who had fallen on bad times, or a professional panhandler?

One last bit of information, or another clue that was presented, was this: After waiting for about ten minutes for his return, and while watching him through my rearview mirror, I saw him get into his truck, start it up, and begin to leave. But being on a dead-end traffic lane with no outlet, he was forced to cut through an empty space between rows and drive past the front of my car to leave. While passing in front of me, he pulled up to where he could speak to me without leaving his vehicle. He said that he had called his wife, who then had called the mission, and they were going to help him get home. Then he drove away.

With that, this story has gone as far as I can take it, but there is one other thing I would like to know: Do you think he went to the mission or just moved on to a new location to practice his trade?

It would be wonderful to find that he had gone to the mission and learned he could have a better life if he would put God first in his life, through God's Son, Jesus Christ.

> *Trust in the LORD with all thine heart; and lean not unto thine own understanding. In all thy ways acknowledge him, and he shall direct thy paths* (Proverbs 3:5–6).

CHAPTER 30

Someone is Always Watching

While I was a young child, around six years old, my parents chose to leave our home in Kansas and move to Mississippi. This move seemed like an excellent adventure to me, and I could hardly wait until we actually got into the old 1950s-model Ford Woody Wagon to move on. The car had seats for five people, and the challenge was that I was person number six. As we loaded into the car, Dad and Mom sat in the front seat and my brothers Eldon and Paul and sister Nancy sat in the remaining seat. That left room for our clothing and everything else that we were taking with us, including me, in the cargo space. It was a fun trip for me as a little boy, because I got to lie on top of everything and I could see out of the top of most all the windows in the car. I was into trying to read road signs to keep track of where we were on a map that I had been given.

There was one recurring sign that really fascinated and frightened me, which read, "Caution, Speed Radar Enforced." This was in the early '50s, when there were Civil Defense shelters everywhere, so if America was attacked with an atomic bomb, we might be able to escape the radiation poisoning. With all this radar going around, I imagined that we probably would be dead before we arrived in Mississippi. Another thing was that all this seemed like an invasion of my privacy, with others being able to see with their radar just how fast we were going, and if they could know that about us, they could probably also see what we were doing. I did not like that at all, but much to my joy we did arrive in Mississippi alive without any apparent lasting effects from the radar radiation, even though some may think I have acquired some fried wiring or something to that effect. Now you can know why I am the way I am.

Fast forward sixty-plus years. We have become accustomed to almost everything we do being recorded on someone's security camera, or perhaps we are being followed by an unmanned drone, or tracked by our smart phone, not to mention all the security cameras we see along the interstates and other highways, as well as overhead cameras at traffic lights in almost all cities. How can we as a society be able to pay for the time of all those people who watch us do everything? When will they have time to live their own lives if they spend their time watching me?

Speaking to a group of young people one Sunday evening on how Jesus knows all about us, I illustrated the point with Bible stories like the one of the Samaritan woman at the well, and how Jesus told her of her five husbands and that she was currently living with another man.

Another story was about a man named Nathanael: *Jesus saw Nathanael coming to him, and saith of him, Behold an Israelite indeed, in whom is no guile! Nathanael saith unto him, Whence knowest thou me? Jesus answered and said unto him, Before that Philip called thee, when thou wast under the fig tree, I saw thee. Nathanael answered and saith unto him, Rabbi, thou art the Son of God; thou art the King of Israel. Jesus answered and said unto him, Because I said unto thee, I saw thee under the fig tree, believest thou? thou shalt see greater things than these. And he saith unto him, Verily, verily, I say unto you, Here-*

after ye shall see heaven open, and the angels of God ascending and descending upon the Son of man (John 1:47–51).

A girl around eleven or twelve years old raised her hand. In all seriousness she asked, "Does Jesus see everything that I do in the bathroom?" A hush fell over the congregation, while they were looking to see and hear my answer to that most compelling question. After all, the girl had a right to know! I have learned that the time to ask the Lord for wisdom is at times like this, and that I can pray without falling to my knees, folding my hands, or closing my eyes. This was one of those times that without fanfare, I needed an immediate answer to that simple question I had never considered before, and praise be to God, He gave me an immediate answer. This is what came out of my mouth: "The Bible tells us in John 1:1–3 that there wasn't anything made without His having a part in it, including making men and women. He made them just like He wanted them to be. Because of this, no matter what you may be doing, Jesus will be saying, 'Great! Everything is working just exactly like I wanted it to!'" Not only could I feel the relief in my soul, I could hear the sigh of relief from the congregation, along with seeing their smiles of satisfaction for a simple answer to a very difficult question. The girl also seemed satisfied with the answer, and praise be to the Lord, we were able to move on without any more discussion on that subject.

Yes indeed, Jesus does know us and everything that we have ever done or will do, and even with all that information, He loves us. Scripture tells us: *"But God commendeth [proved] his love toward us, in that, while were yet sinners, Christ died for us* (Romans 5:8). This tells us that even though He knows who we are, He loves us enough to pay for our eternal salvation.

There was a woman who came into a service station the other day, and she was ahead of me at the cold-drink machine. I couldn't help but notice what was written in ink from one shoulder to the other in large print that was easy to read. It said, "Only God Can Judge Me." As she turned to leave, I told her that I couldn't help but notice the statement that was written on her back. That seemed to gain her attention, so I proceeded to tell her more. I told her that a statement like that was not entirely accurate according to the book that tells us a lot about God. The Bible tells us: *For if we would judge ourselves, we should not be judged* (1 Corinthians 11:31). To simply explain it, God is the judge, but if we will judge ourselves according to His standards, that we are sinners in need of being forgiven, He will forgive and cleanse us, as written in His Word: *If we say that we have no sin, we deceive ourselves, and the truth is not in us. If we confess our sins, he is faithful and just to forgive us our sins, and to cleanse us from all unrighteousness. If we say that we have not sinned, we make him a liar, and his word is not in us* (1 John 1:8–10).

Yes, Jesus is always watching, and because He loves us, He did not come to condemn us, but to be our Savior if we will accept His free gift of salvation by calling on Him.

CHAPTER 31

Blood Work

What is the good word for the day?" asked a nurse as I was waiting for the rest of the day and night to pass after having had a heart catheterization resulting in the installation of a stent. Because of that, I would be spending at least one night in the hospital for observation. So while there, I was working on a project.

A man gave me a box of Bibles to give to others in my travels to rescue missions. While going through them to see what was there, I came across two Bibles that were alike, except for the color of their covers. Even though not broken down, both Bibles testified to much use. They both had a name embossed on the cover. The presentation page in the lady's Bible did not have anything written on it, but the presentation page of the man's Bible contained some information. It was a Christmas gift given to him by the person whose name was on the woman's Bible. This made me curious about the woman who loved the man enough to give him a Bible for Christmas, and want one like his for herself. Knowing neither person, and not wanting to ask a lot of questions, I decided the best way to know about her was to look in her Bible to see what Scriptures she might have marked.

I found it to be a rewarding search, with many portions of Scripture marked, and when the nurse came in, I was in the process of looking at the pages to see if they had any marks. By the time she asked me the question, I was almost through with the initial search. Having read all that was marked, I had begun to form a strong opinion about the lady whose Bible I was searching. In response to the question the nurse had asked, which had caught me completely off guard, I paused for a few moments to reflect on what I was finding. I replied, "Actually, this Bible belonged to a lady I have never met. At my sister's funeral, the minister had taken her Bible and prepared his message based on some of the verses she had highlighted, and by doing this he was able to describe to the letter the sister I had known for sixty-seven years. So I came to the conclusion that if I looked in a person's Bible, I could at least learn what kind of person they wanted to be, and the good word for this day is that the Lord is teaching me about the legacy of a godly person, and I need to leave such a legacy myself." The nurse was pressed for time and had finished what she came in to do, so while leaving, she thanked me for sharing this with her.

A different nurse came in later, and seeing the Bible on the table, asked me a little about what I did. Praise be to God, I was then able to share the legacy story with her too. We briefly discussed the difference between religion and believing in Jesus as our hope of heaven, and touched lightly on several different subjects, including the procedure I had experienced that day. I am not quite sure how it came up, but I told her about the open-heart surgery I had done over eleven years ago. Even though at first, after the doctor explained to me what he would do the next day and how limited I would be in my activities after the surgery, he must have seen the worried look on my face, because he then quickly told me, "Don't worry, Mr. Nance. Ninety percent of the people who have this done come right through it." Now I really had something to worry about; the other ten percent probably die! That did not seem like very good odds to me.

As soon as he left the room, I picked up my Bible from the table and began looking for some relief for the anxiety that was now beginning to grip me, or was it raw fear? In any case, when looking in the concordance for a verse, I came across the Scripture, *Let not your heart be troubled: ye believe in God, believe also in me. In my Father's house are many mansions: if it were not so, I would have told you. I go to prepare a place for you. And if I go and prepare a place for you, I will come again, and receive you unto myself; that where I am, there ye may be also* (John 14:1–3). While reading this and thinking about every word, I came to the realization that the next day I was going to be a better man. Either my heart would have a temporary fix, or I would be with the Lord. In either case, I had nothing to be afraid of, and the joy of the Lord replaced my fear that day.

Later, a young lady came in to get some of my blood. By now I was getting a little leery of another stranger wanting to stick a sharp object into my body. To make it worse, she was doing a lot of searching, as if she wasn't quite sure of herself, even switching arms to look for an easier location. After she had stuck the needle into my arm and had come up without any blood, the fishing expedition began. Trying not to alarm her since, after all, she still had a needle stuck into my arm, I calmly and softly said, "Usually when someone tries to draw blood from me and is unable to get it in the beginning, the only thing that happens when they go fishing is that I get a big bruise and they come up without any blood."

At this point she asked me if she should pull the needle out. My response, while calmly smiling, was, "I think that would be good." Next she asked me if she could try my other arm. (The coward within me was screaming, "No way!") My response was, "If you know you can succeed, go for it. I believe that you can do it!" With a little boost of confident encouragement, she was successful in her search for blood.

While she was finishing, one of the other nurses I had spoken to came in and said that this young lady who was drawing blood (she was in pre-med school and wanted to become a doctor) had been telling her other patients that the nurse who just came into my room really seemed to be a pleasant and happy person. I then told the student that I knew why; it was because she had the love of Jesus in her. The student then said that she was a Muslim. The other nurse then said to me, "Tell her the story you told me, when you had heart surgery and were worried."

WOW! What an opportunity to witness to a Muslim, by just telling her what had happened to me. Quoting John 14:1–3, I explained each part, along with the difference between my God and hers, and finished with verse six, the answer to Thomas's question about where Jesus was going and how he could get there: *Jesus saith unto him, I am the way, the truth, and the life: no man cometh unto the Father, but by me.* As the student was quietly listening, paying close attention to what was being said, I told her that this Jesus loved her every bit as much as He loved me, and He did the "blood work" for us by paying for our sins with His own blood. At this point, she thanked me – hopefully it was for sharing the truth – and then she had to move on.

The other nurse was waiting to give me my evening meds, as we were both rejoicing at the opportunity the Lord had given us to witness to a lost person whom He had sent our way. If she had successfully drawn blood on her first try, I would never have been given that opportunity.

Amazingly enough, my arm was not bruised from the fishing expedition, and all is well.

Isn't God good – all the time?

It is all about the blood of Jesus.

CHAPTER 32

Walking in the Dark

Part 1

Over sixty years ago, I was involved in an unforgettable hunt in the pine forests near Chunky, Mississippi, a small town about fifteen miles east of Meridian.

This was heaven for an adventuresome boy who liked exploring in the woods, enjoying the tall pine trees with a carpet of needles under them, as well as the areas with smaller trees that had vines almost completely covering them. There were many small hills and valleys with some creeks that had clean, clear running water in them, complete with fish, crawdads, turtles, as well as some good swimming holes. The woods were also home for some larger animals, snakes of every size and description, lizards (a boy's best friend), squirrels, including some flying ones, rabbits, and, believe it or not, my dad told us that there were bobcats, wolves, and maybe a panther or two, so we should be very careful, especially at night.

We were living in Mississippi because Dad and Mom wanted my two brothers Eldon and Paul and our sister Nancy to go a Christian school, while they worked at a hospital/sanatorium and on the farm.

The place was called Pine Forest Academy. Several families lived there, each having their own house around a large clearing that included the schoolhouse and church. Because of the nature of the place, there were several children, mostly a little older than I was. We often played in the clearing in the middle. It was mostly covered with sand, an excellent place for barefooted children to play. This was a very special and fun place to be.

We kids were gathered together one afternoon when someone came up with this wildly exciting idea: Let's go snipe hunting! Even though I knew nothing of snipe hunting, or snipes for that matter, it sounded like something I would really like to do. Someone came up with a gunny sack (a burlap sack for animal feed or potatoes), and that was all that was needed.

We headed off down the hill going past the sawmill, the sugarcane press and molasses cooking vat, some horse and mule pens, and the barn. After this large clearing, we continued through some woods on a cart trail that led to and around the side of a cornfield to another cart trail into a hay meadow.

We walked across the meadow to a foot trail that led through another wooded area and ended at a lake that we liked to swim in, but today we would not be swimming. We continued on through the woods for quite a ways until finally we decided we had gone far enough. We were now in sort of a valley that perhaps had been a meadow at one time, but now it had one really big tree and quite a few smaller trees in it. It was decided by the snipe hunting committee that perhaps this would be the place to set the trap.

After some discussion, in which I was just a listener, it was decided that I would be the best person to be left holding the bag. (I would later learn what that phrase actually meant.)

Then they explained to me what an important job that was and how I probably was just the guy to do it. All I had to do was get on my knees beside the big tree and hold the mouth of the bag open so that when they went into the woods, they would drive the snipe toward the tree, and it would just run into the bag to hide from them. Then I could close the bag and we would have the snipe. It sounded easy enough to me, as well as being a great honor to be trusted with such an important job, considering that I was the youngest among them.

I still had a few questions before assuming the hunting position, and before they went out into the woods to drive the snipe back to the bag. What did a snipe look like? Were they dangerous? Did they bite or claw you? What color were they? And what were we going to do with it or them?

I began to wonder if they knew very much about snipes themselves because I didn't get straight answers from anyone. The answers, however, in order, were: They are something between a squirrel or raccoon or possum; no one they knew had ever been hurt by one; even though they had both teeth and claws, they were mostly afraid of people and just wanted a place to hide; and they were perhaps gray, brown, tan, spotted, or striped, except for those with one solid color. The last question was never really answered (What were we going to do with them?) because we couldn't have pets and we were vegetarians. So I figured no one had ever seen or caught one.

It was now late afternoon, so it was time for the hunt to begin. Promising to be very quiet, I assumed the position beside the tree while holding the bag on the ground with the mouth open. As the others were walking away, they were talking quietly and laughing a lot. I kinda hated being left alone there by the tree holding the bag, waiting for something that I couldn't quite imagine, while they were telling some funny story. After all, I liked funny stories as well as anyone else. They continued to walk, and after a while I couldn't hear them at all. I suspected that they were now quietly spreading out to encircle the snipe (What if there were more than the bag would hold?), so I quietly waited and waited and waited. Even though I did not want to miss the rush of the snipes, my knees were hurting, my back was aching, and my arms were tired. So I stood up and listened carefully. I could not hear anything but an occasional stirring in the woods.

Now it was beginning to be dusk, so I started to worry about them! Maybe they were lost, or something happened that they had to go home, so I started calling out to them. There was no answer – not a sound. Now I needed to take action, so I went in the direction that they had gone, still calling out, but there was no answer. I was beginning to panic, as I was very lost. The sun was going down, and I couldn't even find the big tree or the sack. What could I do? What should I do?

Going in circles would not work, so I had to try to walk in a straight direction toward where I thought home would be. I was almost sure that it was in the direction of the sunset, but now it was really beginning to get dark. I continued walking, tripping over things and running into tree limbs and things. Finally, I tripped over a dead tree or something and rolled into a small ravine. That probably was my lowest point emotionally. I got up and carefully crawled out of there. Now I really didn't know where I was going. If I could only see a light somewhere; it would be so much safer if I had some light. I wouldn't be as afraid of some animal getting me.

Either I was getting adjusted to the darkness, or the sky began to yield some light, because I could make out a pine tree whose branches came close enough to the ground that I could climb it. After carefully climbing a ways up, I was able to see a single light glistening occasionally through the trees off in the distance. Returning to the ground, I began walking in the direction of the light. Even though it was still quite a distance off and out of sight most of the time, I was getting closer, and eventually came to a little house where an elderly couple lived.

I do not remember exactly what happened then, but somehow they got me home.

There were at least three things I learned because of this experience:

1. To be left holding the bag means that I am trusting in something unreliable.

2. To be left in the dark means that I did not bring a light.

3. To be lost and without direction means that I should have brought a compass and a map.

CHAPTER 33

Walking in the Dark

Part 2

After a short year or two, I began another journey into the dark, except this time it was spiritual darkness. Almost everyone I knew tried to teach me right from wrong. In school we memorized Scripture, including the Ten Commandments. My dad went around the area holding Bible studies. He had a big reel-to-reel tape player with a slide projector mounted on it. There was also a box of recorded studies with illustration slides that he had purchased. Dad, my two brothers Eldon and Paul, and I would take these things to different houses that had electricity (some houses didn't) and present these studies. Eldon and Paul would carry the big black case containing the tape player, projector, and cords. The case itself was the speaker cabinet. Dad would carry the projector screen and his Bible, and I would carry the box with the tapes and slides. To see us walking in line down the trails or roads would probably remind you of the children of Israel heading for the Promised Land.

When faced with the temptation to do wrong, in all my foolishness, and even with all my training, I would usually fall for the wrong.

Somehow I thought it wouldn't be that big of a deal to try things, and after broadening my knowledge, I just wouldn't continue to do wrong; and besides, God would forgive me.

Corn was planted on the farm, and Eldon and Paul were at another Bible academy, so we were short of workers to hoe the corn. We did not have a cultivator that the horses or mule team could pull through standing crops, so Dad hired a young man from town to help me get the weeds out of the corn. On those hot summer days, we would head to the field in his car. After parking it in the shade on the side of the field, we would go hoe a few rows of corn, and then come back to the car, listen to the radio, and he would smoke a Camel cigarette. He would always ask me if I wanted one, and at first I told him no. After several days of this, and smelling that fresh tobacco and smoke, I eventually decided to try one. It really made me cough at first, but there was a little buzz that made me feel kinda good. It didn't take long before I wanted more and looked for every chance to smoke. I tried almost everything there was, but for the most part, the buzz and satisfaction were gone, but the coughing was not.

We moved back to Kansas by the time I was thirteen, and there I met some new friends. Another teenager I went to school with lived about one block from our apartment. We usually went to and from school together and hung out at his house after school. They had a television and we did not. *The Three Stooges* was usually on, and I believe we used that as a training film. One day after tiring of TV my friend had this brilliant idea: We would take a couple bottles of his dad's beer. He probably wouldn't notice the missing bottles because he was usually drunk when he came home after a hard day at a tavern.

We took the beer to the walled drainage ditch that ran through town across the street from his house. No one would see us in the tall weeds there. He had brought a bottle opener, so he opened both bottles and we each took a sip. It tasted awful, like rotten apples or something. This wasn't his first time drinking beer, so he wasn't having any trouble drinking it, but I was. I just kept sipping and swallowing, trying not to be sick. Cigarettes didn't even seem to help, but I kept trying to force it down. I was starting to feel a little buzz, but then I got sick and lost it all. I couldn't understand how anyone could ever like that slop, but in time it got ahold of me. Any time I would think that I shouldn't be doing these things, I would reason with myself that it was probably too late, because I was such a sinner that I would probably go to hell someday anyway, so I may as well relax and do whatever I wanted to do.

By the time I was sixteen, I had moved to Kansas City and was living in a hotel at Twenty Seventh and Troost, not a very nice or safe place to live, even in the early '60s.

I had a couple of regular jobs and I thought I was doing all right. Living this far away from my parents or anyone else who really cared what I did, I continued further into spiritual darkness.

The day finally came when I wrecked my car and was so bruised that I couldn't work for a couple of weeks, so by then I had lost my jobs. By now I was seventeen and decided to try to join the Navy. They accepted me, but it was going to be a couple of months before I was to go to San Diego, California. I went back to my parents' house in Buffalo, Kansas, where they now lived, and anticipated going on this great adventure to see the world. The Navy was advertising, "Join the Navy and See the World," and that is what I wanted to do. It didn't work out as I had hoped, because after boot camp I spent the remainder of my active Navy time cruising up and down the West Coast on a reserve training ship. This was not what I was looking for, but I discovered that the darkness of sin can be found anywhere you go.

It was probably a blessing from God that I was assigned to that ship, or I probably would have ended up in Vietnam.

During all this time, I had never found that one thing that satisfied the hunger in my soul, so I just kept looking in all the wrong places. After honorably fulfilling my military obligation, I thought that traveling in the United States as an over-the-road truck driver might satisfy that restless longing I had. I did that for several years until it was inconvenient to continue traveling that way. Then my life changed in a major way that I hoped would last forever: I met the girl that I wanted to marry.

Rebecca and I were married on May 17, 1969. Fourteen months later, we had our first son.

With Rebecca and our son James, I felt that life should now be complete, and that longing for something more would go away, but it did not. Yes, a wife and child made my life more fulfilling, and I needed to focus my life on being a good husband and father, so I left the road and worked locally as a mechanic so I could spend more time at home.

There was still a shroud of darkness over my life, and I was afraid that if I were to die, which we all do sooner or later, I would surely go to hell, because I had all this sin in my life that the devil kept reminding me of, and that I didn't know what to do about.

A friend saw me in this distress and asked me what the problem was. I simply told her that I was afraid I was going to die and go to hell. She told me that Jesus was the answer for her when she had felt that way. I listened to what she had to say, which all sounded too good to be true. That night when I went to bed, I couldn't go to sleep, so finally I got up and knelt beside the bed to pray. I remember the words that I said in my heart: *Jesus, I am not even sure that you are really real, but if you are, I am asking you to let me know.* WOW! Immediately a peace and joy filled my life, something I had never experienced before. It was clear to me that Jesus was real, so I told Him that if He would show me what I needed to do, I would try to do it. I will end by simply saying that He did, so I did.

Things have never been the same. I know that I am still not everything I am going to be, but I thank God that I am not what I used to be. I have come out of darkness into the light. I have since learned more about the light, especially with the help of the following verses:

> *Jesus saith unto him, I am the way, the truth, and the life: no man cometh unto the Father, but by me* (John 14:6).

> *Thy word is a lamp unto my feet, and a light unto my path* (Psalms 119:105).

I have learned over the past thirty-eight years that Jesus is what was missing in my life while I was walking in darkness, falling into many of the traps the devil had set for me. All that he ever had to offer was grief and death, since he was eternally separated from God in eternal darkness.

I thank God that Jesus is now the light of my life, and His Word, the Bible, is my map and compass. No longer do I wander around in darkness, not being quite sure of my eternal destination. Looking back to the snipe hunt many years ago reminds me of my wandering around in spiritual darkness, with the devil leaving me to hold an empty bag. What a cruel trick.

CHAPTER 34

Advice from a Cardiologist

Because of a congestive heart condition, it was necessary for me to have open-heart surgery about twelve years ago. The surgeon told me what they had found from having a heart cauterization the day before. It was the worst news I had ever had regarding my health and physical future. I was told that my heart was circulating around only twenty percent of the blood that it should be, and because of the extended time it had been in this condition, surgery would likely only bring it back to something like forty percent.

I refused to believe that would be the case, so after the surgery and completion of therapy, I tried to go back to work in my woodworking factory as if nothing had ever happened. After all, as a pastor of a small church, I needed to be bi-vocational in order to survive financially. I realized that there were many more churches in America that could not financially support their pastors than there were that could, so to be an effective church worker or leader, I must do whatever was necessary, and working in another occupation along with the ministry was essential.

After about three years of trying as hard as I could, I came to the grim realization that the doctor probably knew what he was talking about, and something had to change. Now, at fifty-nine years old, with a serious physical impairment, the likelihood of me finding gainful employment was not high. After exhausting almost all of our resources and extending our credit to the breaking point, I was forced to do something that to me was unthinkable. My pride in being able to take care of myself was also about to be broken, and there was nothing I could do to change that, so I applied for Social Security disability payments.

Those at the Social Security office seemed to think that my case was documented enough that there would be no problem in processing the claim. It seems that we were all in some kind of dream world, because the claim was flatly denied. I took the matter to an attorney. We appealed their decision and were granted a hearing before a judge. This was great news, but there was one larger-than-life problem: there was a two-year backlog on hearings. We would have to somehow just get by.

My good friend Jesse Cass encouraged me to go to the Veterans Administration and ask for my medical benefit which, admittedly, I didn't know that I had. Because of having honorably fulfilled my military obligation by serving four years' active duty in the Navy, I was entitled to receive total veterans' health benefits, including medication. This was a great relief in that my medications were costing around three hundred dollars each month. Times really were tough, and without Rebecca's work, a few ministry opportunities, and the blessings of the Lord, I don't know how we could have survived. The Social Security disability hearing was finally held.

One of their doctors had reviewed my case, and the attorney, doctor, the judge, and Rebecca and I met for the hearing at a motel hearing room in Chillicothe, Missouri. Most of the discussion held at the hearing was between the doctor and the judge. The doctor was spending a lot of time telling the judge what I would no longer be able to do and that I was too old for occupational rehabilitation. After a few more questions and comments by everyone there, we were dismissed with the promise that in a few weeks we would learn of the judge's verdict.

The benefit was granted, and eventually the money came in, which was greatly appreciated. The back pay didn't begin to cover our accumulated debts, but it was a great turning point toward recovery.

Throughout this whole process, I had been speaking at several rescue missions each month, witnessing many people make decisions to give their lives to Jesus or recommit their lives to Him. Over the years, I had added a few places to speak each month and really wanted to do more, but I didn't know how that would be possible. Again, my friend Jesse Cass came to the rescue. He had some friends at the Missouri Baptist Convention, and he appealed to them to consider supporting the *Sparrow Ministry*. Under the direction of Dr. Danny Decker, who was over men's ministries at the time, they began helping us on a monthly basis, which caused the ministry to grow from reaching hundreds a year to reaching thousands. Over the years, they have fallen on hard times and have cut their support in half, but by the grace of God and His followers, some of whom are partners with us in reaching souls for Christ, the ministry continues to grow, and as we wait for the return of Christ, I intend to continue serving as long as God allows.

To understand the advice from the cardiologist, it was necessary to fill in what was happening in my life, from heart surgery to this most recent procedure, where I was thoroughly checked out and had a stent installed in a mostly blocked vein. The procedure went well and seems to be effective.

On a follow-up visit about one month after the procedure, the cardiologist said that my heart was performing at around ninety percent, so I should keep doing what I had been doing for the past ten years.

> *Trust in the LORD with all thine heart; and lean not unto*
> *thine own understanding. In all thy ways acknowledge him,*
> *and he shall direct thy paths* (Proverbs 3:5–6).

The greatest blessing in my life was accepting Jesus Christ as my Lord and Savior and beginning to live for Him. This heart problem was a blessing because it put me in a place where all I could do was serve Him. Being reduced to, or more correctly, being lifted into being a servant of the Most High God, is the highest calling anyone can ever have in their life. Being rich in the Spirit brings peace, joy, and satisfaction that money cannot buy.

These are available to all who will trust and follow Jesus the Savior.

CHAPTER 35

Repellant

Being a missionary evangelist causes me to go to some places I would rather not go to because of weather conditions, extreme heat or cold, and in some cases, other considerations such as health hazards. While planning my monthly trip to Shreveport and Dallas, the West Nile Virus was on the news most of the time. If I were to listen to my fears, or what some would call common sense, some friendly advisers would say, "Why not skip this trip at least for September and wait for all this to calm down, as mosquito season will be drawing to a close." This made good sense to me, so I would at least pray about not going.

When praying about something, I try to open my heart and hear from God, while openly admitting that some time is spent trying to convince God that I have valid reasons not to go to the places that I have agreed to go to. Then the question usually arises in my heart, Why would I go there to begin with? The answer to that question is overwhelmingly simple: I am a missionary evangelist who, I feel, has been called by God to take the message of salvation through Jesus to the largest accumulation of people that may not know of Jesus as their only hope of salvation. Many others think that this life is all there is, and the truth is that we will all live eternally at one place or the other, heaven or hell. Without choosing Jesus as our way to heaven, we will certainly end up in hell, whether we believe that or not. Because of these facts, and the urgency of the message, I must go wherever people that have not submitted themselves to Jesus' salvation are, whether I feel safe in going or not.

In preparing for this trip, I purchased a big spray can of mosquito repellant to douse myself with, and, hopefully, if they came looking for lunch, they would either drown in it or slide off before they were able to drill for blood. Equipped with a full can of repellant, I would probably survive.

Also in preparation for this trip I purchased a large spray bottle of bed bug killer. While traveling for Jesus in the last few years, I have encountered another bug He created that also has a hearty appetite for my blood. It is hard for me to understand just why Jesus would make such a bug as that, but I am sure He has his reasons, so I must just try to equip myself to keep it as far from me as possible. I suppose I have been the main course at their dinner three times or so. It is not that I would begrudge them a few drops of blood; testing my blood sugar often causes me to shed plenty of it anyway. It is just that bed bugs and mosquitos leave you with all that itching and the potential for infections and diseases. Of course, whether I am traveling or not, I would like to stay as healthy as possible for as long as possible. So while traveling, I try to be prepared for these possible hazards.

I was able to make it to Shreveport with only minimal exposure to these possible pests by spending the first night in the *sparrowmobile* with the windows closed and a little bug spray on, just in case they had snuck in somehow. Fortunately, I had spent most of that first night driving with the air conditioner on because it was in the eighties that night. When I did need rest, it would take the car about an hour to be too warm to sleep, so that worked out great. After speaking in Shreveport that Wednesday evening, I intended to spend another night in the car, hiding from the potential bed bugs, at a nice rest area on the east edge of Texas.

On the way to the rest area, it was around a hundred degrees, so to kill a little time while it cooled down, I stopped at the Golden Arches and stayed until they closed the place at eleven o'clock that night. Coming out of there into the night, I expected it to be somewhat cooler, but it was still in the nineties. I drove the few miles to the rest area, thinking that since it was dark, it would be no hotter in the car than it was outside, so I tried to be as comfortable as possible. I thought I could sleep even through the heat because I was very tired. As a thinking person might expect, it wasn't working. Perhaps it wasn't any hotter in the car than it was outside, but it was way too hot to get any rest. The only solution would be to go to a motel and offer myself as a living sacrifice for the nourishment of the little creatures.

It was after midnight when I came to what appeared to be a user-friendly motel that wouldn't cost an arm and a leg, perhaps just a finger or two, so I checked in. The room was clean and didn't smell of smoke, so I believed I had made a wise decision. First, I brought in the bug killer and repellant and then went hunting for bed bugs everywhere. Even though there were none to be seen, you could be safe in saying that I treated the whole room with the killer spray, hoping that it didn't work on humans. Next, I brought in my bag and clothing, treating them for bugs, as well as treating the place where I would keep them that night. By now I was so tired that I took off my shoes, lay down on the bed, and drifted off to sleep, while asking the Lord to protect me from all harm in the night and thanking Him for providing such a comfortable place to stay. Later, I woke up enough to actually get into bed as I should. It didn't take long to fall into a deep sleep, because the next thing I was thinking about was an annoying noise, and I finally realized that it was my phone ringing.

It was my favorite daughter Angie (I only have one) returning my call. I must have called her in my sleep, because I didn't remember calling. She said that she had not made it to the phone in time, so she was calling me back. Since she was now on the phone, and I like talking to her whether I plan to or not, we talked for about an hour. By now it was past nine o'clock in the morning, and light was shining in around the curtain. I was still lying in bed when I saw a Texas-sized MOSQUITO!!! While holding the cell phone in one hand so I could tell her if it attacked me, and grabbing the repellant with the other, I got up and fogged it real good. When the fog cleared, I could not find even the remains of the mosquito. I went over my exposed body looking for itchy spots, and there were none. I was so tired that I had forgotten to use the repellent.

I have said all this so that I can give credit to where credit is due: It was the Lord who protected me, not the repellant. Instantly a very familiar truth came to me: *Trust in the LORD with all thine heart; and lean not unto thine own understanding. In all thy ways acknowledge him, and he shall direct thy paths* (Proverbs 3:5–6).

It was the Lord who protected me.

My friend Larry, who has gone on to be with the Lord, told me on several occasions, "Earl, the Lord takes care of you because you are too ignorant to take care of yourself." Once again, Larry was correct.

CHAPTER 36

Father's Love

One afternoon I stopped at our house in Kansas City, Missouri, to check on our children. I don't remember why they weren't with their grandmother that afternoon, where they usually were after school, but I do remember that I needed to either check on them or take them somewhere. Mike was around nine years old, and Angie was around thirteen. In that they were as trustworthy as children of that age are, we thought they could be alone at home for a short time without trouble or without hurting one other. This was over twenty-five years ago, and it was a much different time in America.

Upon going into the house, I found that there was a contest going on at the door to the boy's room. Angie was in the hall, and Mike was in his room, either trying to get out or trying to keep Angie from coming in. I did not know exactly what it was all about, but it seemed to all be in fun, so, unbeknownst to Mike, I joined in by holding the knob tightly so Mike could no longer turn it. Before long I heard a few words that I had become very familiar with as a sailor. I had not said anything yet, and Mike still did not know I was home, but now I was forced to say something.

I said, "Mike, you should not talk like that." I then let go of the doorknob, and I guess that he did also, because now there was no one trying to come out of or go into his room. Angie was also very quiet, looking like she was worried about Mike's fate. After all, she was his big sister and was commissioned to be his fearless protector. How was she now going to protect him from me?

Quietly walking to the living room, I sat down on the couch so I could see his door down the hall. Surely he would come out of his room before long, if just to clean himself up or get a drink of water. He could not stay in there for the rest of his life! To get out of our house, one would either have to climb out of the windows or come through the living room. Eventually Mike's door slowly opened and he stepped into the hall, stepping so softly one would almost think that he was walking on eggshells, trying not to break them. As he came into the living room, I calmly and quietly told him to sit down on the couch. I was not sure that Mike and Angie were still breathing. It was so quiet that I could almost hear their hearts beating. After waiting a few moments to let their imaginations carry them away, I told them that I was going to tell them a story.

The story began by my telling them, "When I was about your age, Mike, my sister Nancy took me to a go-cart track one day and left me there with two dollars, so that I could ride the carts while she went to see a friend (probably a boy). Dad and Mom would make her take me with her when she would take our car. I suppose it was so she wouldn't do anything that she shouldn't do in her little brother's presence. What Dad didn't know was that for a couple of dollars' hush money, my lips were sealed. She usually took me to the skating rink, a friend's house, or the go-cart track until she had done whatever she had set out to do, and then would come back and we'd go home together.

On this particular day, I had just begun cruising around the track, having a lot of fun, and I still had enough money to take a few more rides, when I saw the big green Buick come into the parking lot. Nancy jumped out, came to the fence, and started waving to me frantically. While wondering what had gone wrong, I begrudgingly parked the cart at the end of that lap before my time was up. She just told me to hurry up and get into the car. When I asked her what went wrong or what the problem was, she would not tell me. She looked as though she was almost paralyzed with fear. Then I asked if everyone was okay. She simply said that they were, but we had to go home. I began saying things about Dad, like calling him a crazy old coot, and, much to my surprise, Nancy had nothing to say this time but was looking more ghostly and stressed by the minute. She was driving as though her life depended on it and not saying a word. I kept complaining about Dad until we stopped by the outside stairs that went up to our apartment, which was over a furniture store. As I was getting out of the car I noticed, for the first time, my dad sitting in the back seat.

I was terrified, thinking that my end had come and I was about to die. Without saying a word, I went up to our living room and sat on the couch, waiting for the "death angel" to come.

At this point in the story, I looked Mike in the eye and said to him, "Mike, I am going to do to you exactly what my dad did to me!" It was as if all the air was sucked out of the room and the clocks quit running, because time may have stood still. Mike jerked as though I had struck him.

I got off the couch, went out the front door without saying a word, got in the car, and drove away for a while.

Mike never said anything about what had occurred, but Angie had to know what my dad had done to me, so I told her the rest of the story: "When my dad came into our living room, he walked past me on the couch, not looking at me or saying a word, and went to his room. I did not see him for quite a while." There was never a mention of what had happened or what I had done, and Dad, Mother, and Nancy never will mention it in this life because they have all gone to be with the Lord, but my loving memory of them lives on.

Only a father can love his wayward children like that. I am so thankful my earthly father taught me what my heavenly Father would be like.

> Scripture tells us that *God commendeth [proved] his love toward us, in that, while we were yet sinners, Christ died for us* (Romans 5:8), and *If we confess our sins, he is faithful and just to forgive us our sins, and to cleanse us from all unrighteousness* (1 John 1:9).

Have you received the heavenly Father's love? It is yours for the asking.

CHAPTER 37

Trust the Water

We had a nice lake located down the trail through the tall pine trees. There were other trees laden with Spanish moss, and the beautiful magnolia trees were blooming in their season. This was a few miles south of Chunky, Mississippi, at a school complex called Pine Forest Academy, where my parents had moved our family so my two brothers and sister and I would be in a Christian school. For a young boy in the early 1950s, it was a haven of adventure land.

In trying to remember the size of the lake, I am reminded that someone had a motorboat that was big enough to pull what they called a surfboard. This was unlike the surfboards of today. The board was made from a piece of plywood, probably three quarters of an inch thick and sealed with paint (probably lead-based paint; I'm thankful we were not allowed to chew on it!). It was about three feet wide and five feet long, with all edges rounded. The front was rounded with a hole cut in it so a rope could be tied to it to pull it. Close to the front there was a hole on either side where another rope could be tied to form a loop that the rider could hold on to, making it somewhat possible to stand up, allowing the rider to shift their weight from side to side, giving them a little control of where they wanted to go, as long as they wanted to follow the general direction of the boat. They didn't go very fast, but it looked like a lot of fun.

Someone else had a rowboat that they had fashioned by fastening two car hoods together, end to end, and somehow sealing the point where they were joined together. They had mounted a couple of boards in it for seats. I remember imagining how fulfilled my life would be if I could have nice water rides like these, but adventures such as these were completely out of my reach because I was too young and didn't even know how to swim. I was left to dream of how much fun it must be to be a teenager with all this knowledge.

There was also an elevated pier with a diving board. It was maybe six to eight feet from the board to the water. Everyone who was allowed to use it seemed to be having a great time, but you needed to know how to swim because the water was deep in that part of the lake.

Being afraid of the water, because of not knowing how to swim, I was really limited in the fun I could have had at the lake, even though there was a sandy area used to put boats in the water and as a beach area. The bottom of this sandy area was not very steep, which made it a great place to play for us non-swimmers. In an effort to learn to swim, I would crawl around in the shallow water, hoping to start swimming, but it was not working. When I was not touching the bottom with my feet or hands, I was afraid that I would drown.

At the church we attended a couple times a week, there was a big clock with a sweeping second hand on the wall behind the preacher. (If the congregation was so concerned with the time, why didn't they place the clock where the speaker could clearly see it?) I liked to go to church and was delighted with the placement of the clock, because the clock with its second hand was the only place I could go to see such an accurate measure of time. You may have guessed by now why the measuring of time by seconds was so important to me. It was so that I could practice holding my breath. If I could do that, I could be under water for a little while, while trying to learn to swim. I am sure this was a great cause of irritation to my dad and mom as we sat in church with me taking a deep breath, holding it until my face turned red, and then gasping for air. Having regained my composure, I would do it over and over. Back then I could hold it for well over two minutes. All of this breathing exercise did not bring me any closer to knowing how to swim or of being less afraid of potentially drowning.

An older woman (she must have been around sixteen or seventeen, over twice my age) took an interest in trying to teach the few of us who didn't know how to swim, how to do so.

The first thing she did was take us way out into the deep water. It must have been at least up to my waist. Next, we were to take a deep breath and hold it (that I was already pretty good at), then lie face down flat on the bottom. That sounded a little scary, but she would be right there, so if I didn't come up soon, she would pull me out. Try as I might, I could not lie on the bottom, because every time I tried, one end of me or the other began to float to the surface. It was impossible for me to get my entire body on the bottom at one time and keep it there. I had always thought that the water was going to suck me under and hold me there, but I found that was not true as long as I kept some air in my lungs. What a flotation device! It was ever present if only I would use it.

After learning that I could not stay on the bottom, I quickly learned how to move around while keeping my head out of the water, at least long enough to get another breath. Soon I was swimming with the rest of them, and I could swim farther under water than any of my friends. (That's putting my church learning to use; I would rather that I had been listening and learning truth about the Lord.)

This swimming lesson was so simple, and to learn that it was easier for the water to hold me up than it was to keep me down, as long as I had air in my lungs, made the rest easier to do. Learning to swim left me believing I could do just about anything I wanted to do, as long as it was not in violation of any natural law. (I tried flying from a barn loft, but it didn't work out so well, even though I had a big breath of air until the landing.)

This experience of learning to swim reminds me somewhat of learning to serve the Lord. I was afraid to do that because I might fail. Truth is, whether swimming or serving the Lord, we must be filled to be able to survive. In the water, I must be filled with air, and to survive in the world, I must be filled with the Holy Spirit of God. As the water wants to hold me up, the Holy Spirit also wants to hold me up. Scripture tells us that greater is He that is in us (the Holy Spirit) than he that is in the world (the spirit of antichrist).

> Remember that the Bible tells us: *I can do all things through Christ which strengtheneth me* (Philippians 4:13), and to *Trust in the LORD with all thine heart; and lean not unto thine own understanding. In all thy ways acknowledge him, and he shall direct thy paths* (Proverbs 3:5–6).

CHAPTER 38

New Year's Eve and Early Morning 2012–13

After a great New Year's Eve service at Denver Rescue Mission, where eighteen people decided for Christ, I left Denver, needing to be in Kansas City, Missouri, by the next afternoon.

This had been one of the best New Year's Eve celebrations I have had in my life, second only to the one when I realized that I had been holding out on the Lord, choosing to do only those things I wanted to do. It was kind of like being at a food buffet, going through the line and taking a little or a lot of the things that taste good but may not be good for me, and leaving those healthy choices that don't tantalize my taste. That evening I quit holding out on the Lord and committed my will and life to Him. This evening would not have been possible if I had not made that commitment to the Lord well over thirty years ago. Admittedly, I have had more than my share of failures, but I have no regrets for having made that decision for the Lord, and I hope to never turn back.

It was around 8:00 p.m. as I turned onto Interstate 70 on the way to Kansas City. The temperature had really dropped that evening and was now well below freezing. The road was mostly dry to begin with and traveling was easy, allowing me to make pretty good time. The evening was going well, as I was reflecting on the service that was conducted in Denver, while listening to some enjoyable Southern Gospel music on the new radio/CD player with Pandora capability that my grandson Caleb had just installed in the *sparrowmobile*. After driving for over sixty thousand miles with a CD player that would not work properly, it was relaxing to hear uplifting and beautiful music that praises the Lord. About 10:00 p.m. it seemed like a good time to stop for supper, or dinner, depending on which side of the tracks you are from. It doesn't work too well for me to eat before speaking, and one needs a little cool-off time after the meeting, so the time was right. There was a restaurant ahead that boasted its two-, four-, and six-dollar menu, which is a favorite of mine, so I stopped and had my usual. When it came time to pay the bill, which hadn't come yet, I asked the server for it, and she told me that she hoped I would not be offended, but the people who had been sitting at the next table asked for my ticket and paid it. I felt blessed, because we had not so much as spoken, yet they must have wanted to do at least one more good deed in 2012, and I had been on the receiving end of it. It also allowed me to pass most of the good deed along to the server. With the frosting, as it were, on the end of the year, I got back in the *sparrowmobile* and proceeded eastward, driving into the cold night.

The weather had begun to change for the worse, in that it was now between eight and ten degrees with patchy fog. Knowing that this could develop into a very dangerous situation, I traveled on cautiously, even to the point of reducing my speed somewhat. There were only a few vehicles on the road competing for the available space, mostly trucks, along with a very few regular travelers. The farther I went, the worse the roads were getting. It had snowed in Kansas earlier that day as I was traveling to Denver, and now I was beginning to get to that portion of road that still had some packed snow and icy spots. Finally it was midnight, so I called Rebecca to wish her a happy new year and tell her about the evening's blessings from God.

About an hour and a half into 2013, I was reflecting on the ministry's record-breaking year that the Lord had given me and wondering what this new year could have in store that would possibly come anywhere near as rewarding as the last one. I didn't have long to wait to begin seeing the challenges and rewards of this new year, by first being allowed to assist a man, woman, and infant who were all in great distress and peril.

The road conditions continued to get worse, and by now there was almost no other traffic moving in either direction. As my courage continued to diminish, I turned off the cruise control and radio, so the situation would be more controllable with fewer distractions. Down the road quite a ways, through the patchy fog and light snow, there appeared to be some kind of light some distance to the right of the roadway. As I came closer, it looked like some kind of vehicle next to the fence that was along the side of the right of way. While coming much closer, I determined that indeed it was a vehicle that had left the road, having traveled through a wide ditch and several car lengths up a small hill. It was on its side with the headlights and taillights still on. Gently applying the brake caused me to break traction, and it seemed like I was gaining speed, as is usually the case when you discover you are on black ice. I am not sure, but it seemed as though the rumble strip on the right side of the road helped me to stay on the road as I was slowly coming to a stop. It was about a long city block back to where the distressed vehicle was, so seeing no lights in either direction on the interstate, I backed up the middle of the roadway to the vehicle, stopping as far off the roadway as I could without getting stuck. Getting out of the car, I called out, "Is anybody there?" several times. There was no response, so I got my little flashlight, grabbed my gloves and cell phone, and proceeded down into the wide ditch. It was quite a surprise when the snow immediately was over my knees. I tripped and dropped the flashlight and one of my gloves, and was trying to stand up and find them, when a man's muffled voice began coming from the vehicle calling, "HELP! HELP!"

It was amazing to me how hearing him caused me to make it out of the snowdrift with both the light and glove almost immediately. I called out that I was on my way, and as I came closer to the vehicle, I began to hear a child crying, which struck terror in my heart. I thought that I was going as fast as I could, but this new development moved me a little faster. As I was getting nearer, and bracing myself for the worst, as well as praying for some relief for all of us, the voice within the vehicle said, "Help me get the baby out of here! Take him to your car!" By now I was at the pickup truck. It had rolled multiple times, leaving a trail of debris in its path that included a short camper cover, luggage, and a trail of other things. It ended up with the passenger's side on the ground. The top, which was facing me, was smashed almost to the dash, and all the glass had been broken out of the windows. Immediately, I shined the light down into the back window opening, where it sounded like the baby's voice was coming from, and there he was, on his side, fastened in his car seat, which was securely installed in the truck. Praise God, he seemed to be well, even though he was cold, scared, and shaken up. In the light, the man unfastened the baby and lifted him up out of the window opening, telling me to take him. Even though my hands were full, I got the baby with my arms, holding him closely, trying to share a little warmth with him, as well as affording him a little security. He was still crying, but after brushing the snow out of his hair and putting the little hoodie that was on his pajama outfit over the top of his head and ears, he quit crying and seemed at peace with his new reality.

We were almost to the big snowdrift, and I was wondering how I would get through it with the baby and other things in my hands, but praise the Lord, car lights came over the hill in the distance, coming our way, so I began waving the little light, hoping that they would see it and stop. By now I had been out of my car for around ten minutes and had not seen any other traffic going in either direction. The vehicle did slow down and stop, and the driver got out, so I called out to him, asking him to come get the baby. It was a younger man, who was able to run through the deep snow, taking him back to his SUV. He said that his wife was there, as well as a couple of teenage daughters, and I also asked him to call 9-1-1, which they did. Now that the baby was secure and emergency responders were being called, I went back to the wreck to see what else I could possibly do. Again looking down into the truck through the driver's window opening, I saw a woman lying on the windows, which were now against the ground. The man inside the truck said that she had told him that she couldn't feel anything, nor could she move. I felt so helpless seeing her lying crumpled up inside of this wreck, and there was nothing I could do to help her. The man was still in the vehicle and said that he wanted to stay right there with her until help arrived.

With this, I started back to my car to get another light and a blanket, and as I was going past the SUV, the other man was about to go back to the crash. As we were talking, my feet slipped on the ice, and I landed on my knees, about six feet from his SUV. It was so slick that I could not get up, so he tried to help me, but he was also having a hard time standing up. Finally, I crawled close enough to reach the fender well by the back tire on the SUV. I held on to it, and slid myself close enough to brace against the tire and stand up. Getting it together, while trying to ignore the new pain, I continued back to my car to get the other light. I did find it, but the battery was dead. Can you imagine, three vehicles, including the wreck, and only one little light? What were we all thinking? While waiting in the dark for help, I called 9-1-1 to let them know about the woman and man who were still in the vehicle, and the baby who was safe. I was assured that help was on its way, but it would probably be another ten minutes before they arrived. There was nothing more I could do without light and with banged-up knees, except put on my heavy parka and go to the ditch side of the car in the event that someone else lost control and crashed into it. At least I would be able to fall back into the snow pile. While standing there in the dark, appraising the situation and praying for help, It occurred to me that with the lights still on in the vehicle, that meant the ignition switch probably had not been turned off, so it had all the makings of a bigger tragedy – the potential for an electrical fire. Again, a wave of raw terror gripped me, because none of us was prepared for that potential emergency. Knowing about that possibility, and how to deal with it if I only had a good working fire extinguisher, did nothing to comfort me. I'm thankful that my fears never materialized that night.

At last, the first emergency vehicle arrived, an old ambulance that the volunteer fire department was using. There were three guys in it who jumped out, without lights, and went over to the wreck. The youngest one was running back and forth from their ambulance-van to the wreck getting various things. I couldn't see what they were doing, but next a real ambulance arrived, and they asked them to turn on their side lights because they couldn't see what they were doing. The lights were turned on, and soon after, a law officer came. I do not know if he was a state patrolman or a sheriff. He got out of his car without even a jacket or hat on, and he was not carrying a flashlight either.

After telling him everything I knew about what had happened and what had been done so far, he encouraged me to go ahead and leave, so there would be one less vehicle presenting a hazard, should any other traffic come along. I believe that in all this time, only one truck had come by. I followed his instructions, drove to the first exit with a lighted business, and stopped for the night.

While reflecting the next morning, New Year's morning, on what had occurred and what I could have done differently, I realized two changes must be made to remedy my lack of preparedness. First, I must be prepared for potentially fighting fire, and second, I must have more light available. While thinking about these things and then getting more lights and a fire extinguisher, I realized that in my travels, this is the main message I bring to lost people: that because of what Jesus has done for us, we can choose to escape the eternal fire, and Jesus is the Light that we need to show us the right way.

<u>FIRST.</u> Without Jesus as our Lord and Savior, we are facing eternal flames from which there will be no escape. Jesus tells us: *I am the way, the truth, and the life: no man cometh unto the Father, but by me* (John 14:6). This tells us we will escape the eternal flames with Jesus, so Jesus is my personal eternal fire extinguisher.

<u>SECOND.</u> Jesus tells us in His Word, the Bible: *I am the light of the world: he that followeth me shall not walk in darkness, but shall have the light of life* (John 8:12).

Jesus further explains this in the following verses of Scripture: *For God so loved the world, that he gave his only begotten Son, that whosoever believeth in him should not perish, but have everlasting life. For God sent not his Son into the world to condemn the world; but that the world through him might be saved. He that believeth on him is not condemned: but he that believeth not is condemned already, because he hath not believed in the name of the only begotten Son of God. And this is the condemnation, that light is come into the world, and men loved darkness rather than light, because their deeds were evil. For every one that doeth evil hateth the light, neither cometh to the light, lest his deeds should be reproved. But he that doeth truth cometh to the light, that his deeds may be made manifest, that they are wrought in God* (John 3:16–21).

Dear Reader, you may be asking, How can I know that I have the LIGHT of JESUS in me? Scripture tells us: *That if thou shalt confess with thy mouth the Lord Jesus, and shalt believe in thine heart that God hath raised him from the dead, thou shalt be saved. For with the heart man believeth unto righteousness; and with the mouth confession is made unto salvation. For the scripture saith, Whosoever believeth on him shall not be ashamed. For there is no difference between the Jew and the Greek: for the same Lord over all is rich unto all that call upon him. For whosoever shall call upon the name of the Lord shall be saved* (Romans 10:9–13).

When I was about thirty, a friend told me that I needed to do more than just believe that Jesus was a good teacher who died because of sin. I needed to pray, admitting to Him that I am a sinner in need of His salvation, and believe that God did raise Him from the dead. When I did that, He gave me peace and joy in my heart, replacing the fear of death that had always dogged me.

This experience of being out in the dark without a working light and having nothing to put out a fire if one were to occur, reminded me of those similar feelings that were in my life before I came to JESUS, the ETERNAL LIGHT, and the ONLY WORKING FIRE EXTINGUSHER.

If you have not accepted Jesus as your hope of heaven, please do it now, before it is eternally too late.

To date, I do not know the outcome of the man, woman, and child who were in the wrecked pickup truck. The Kansas Highway Patrol report said that all three were taken to a hospital with injuries and were dismissed or moved, and that is the extent of information available to me. The only thing we can do is pray for them.

CHAPTER 39

New Year's Eve
and Early Morning

2012–13 Continued

In an effort to contact the people in this accident, I took the names, ages, and city they lived in from the accident report the Highway Patrol had posted online. With that information, I did an online people search and found several likely addresses. I then sent the first part of this story to each of them, asking them that if they were the person in the story to please contact me and let me know how they were.

After over two months of wondering and praying, praise and glory be to God, I received a letter from the woman in the wrecked pickup. Following is her letter with the names changed to Jack, Jill, and Junior. I will also omit the name of the city and church they attend, to protect their privacy.

> *Dear Earl,*
>
> *My name is Jill and I am the woman that was in the accident that you came upon the morning of the New Year. Jack received your letter a couple of weeks ago and we were so incredibly touched by it. We never knew who the angel*

was that stopped to help us that frigid-cold night just a few moments after our accident happened and now we know it was you. It was one of our deepest regrets that we never knew your name. We did know the name of the man of the family that stopped right after you, but we never found out his last name either.

First I want to let you know that thankfully and miraculously we are all fine. Jack got some scratches on his face and a bruised foot and I suffered a spinal cord injury. As you know, our son Junior was also unscathed. Immediately following the accident I was paralyzed from the neck down and remained that way for just a little while. There were many angels helping us that night, including yourself and the paramedics and doctors that were at a small hospital about 10 miles away. After a series of x-rays and scans at the hospital, they realized I needed more help than they could provide 7 weeks of recovery in a neck brace, my strength has started to return. I still have numbness and tingling in my arms and hands, but I'm able to do many household chores I couldn't do 4-5 weeks ago. The follow-up surgeon I have here at home is still amazed that I'm even walking, but I do expect to make a full recovery.

Jack and I have reflected on that night so many times and we continue to live in gratitude and grace. Knowing that you're a God-loving man, I'll share with you a little of my experience immediately following the accident. About Blessings to you and yours.

Your friends always,

Jack, Jill, and Junior

What a way to begin the year of 2013. Just a couple of hours into this year, God allowed me to be at the proper place at just the right time. I call these He allows me to be used in His Master plan. It is a very special blessing to ask the Lord for a miracle and find that God granted it, no matter how few or many are praying. This further grounds me in placing all my faith in God, knowing that He cares for us and hears our prayers.

My prayer is that Jack and Jill and their son Junior may use this event as a reminder to always live for the Lord Jesus Christ, the dispenser of mercy and grace. He illustrates once again that our time is in His hands. Every breath we breathe is a gift from Him.

This event caused me to evaluate my preparedness or lack thereof to deal with emergencies that may be encountered in my life, as well as in the lives of others.

I believe Jesus when He said: *I am the way, the truth, and the life: no man cometh unto the Father, but by me* (John 14:6). To get on the right way required a decision on my part to do what is said in God's Holy Word: *That if thou shalt confess with thy mouth the Lord Jesus, and shalt believe in thine heart that God hath raised him from the dead, thou shalt be saved* (Romans 10:9). I believe that, and have confessed with my mouth that belief, so I am confident that my spirit is right with God.

I am now better prepared physically to deal with such an event. We have purchased several lights, blankets, bandages, a fire extinguisher, and other emergency equipment. My prayer is that these things will never need to be used on anyone, including myself.

CHAPTER 40

Trying to Stay Positive

Several months ago at a regular visit to the Veterans Administration, the doctor who is assigned to deal with my many health issues or the lack thereof, noticed something irregular in my throat. Frankly, that came as no surprise, considering the things I have either swallowed or tried to swallow, including both things of substance and sometimes wild ideas. Her point of interest at this visit was one enlarged tonsil. It was almost like she was on a treasure hunt, and any problem, real or perceived, that she discovered was the treasure. I considered her to be an important part of this ministry team, in that she appeared to actually be interested in helping me through the many potential things that could overcome me and cause my ministry to end. I do enjoy life, and the day-to-day living of it, but the truth is, I am confident of my relationship with Jesus, and at the end of this earthly life, I will be in the best part, eternal life with the Lord, our eternal keeper. Until then, though, I am pleased to be in the care of a diligent and knowledgeable doctor who is helping me to spend more time here, while I enjoy telling others of Jesus' mercy, grace, and salvation.

What she discovered caused her to make appointments for me with the CAT scan people, as well as the ear, nose, and throat doctor. The appointments were set for January 3. She seemed very determined to get this done as soon as possible. Because of the rush, as well as some of her questions, I began to imagine all manner of horrible potential problems. Sometimes it would be better not to have seen some of the things that I have seen, along with having such a wild imagination, but sad sometimes to say, this is just who I am.

I had a very aggressive schedule set for that week, and it did not include the VA clinic and hospital in central Missouri, so it was necessary to make some major adjustments. Any time I cannot be at one of my ministry opportunities, I count it as a major adjustment. To understand my dilemma and disappointment in needing to radically cancel part of the ministry opportunities I had agreed to, you need to see my agenda for that week as follows:

Sunday, December 30, 2012, 7:30–8:30 p.m.: Peoria Rescue Mission, Peoria, Illinois

Monday, December 31, 2012, 6:30–7:30 p.m.: Denver Rescue Mission, Denver, Colorado

Tuesday, January 1, 2013, 10:00 a.m.–2:00 p.m.: helping my son James, Kansas City, Missouri

Wednesday, January 2, 2013, 6:30–7:30 p.m.: Rescue Mission, Shreveport, Louisiana

Thursday, January 3, 2013, 6:00–7:00 p.m.: Dallas Life Rescue Mission, Dallas, Texas

Friday, January 4, 2013, 7:00–8:00 p.m.: Highway 80 Rescue Mission, Longview, Texas

The reason for telling you of this schedule is so that you will understand my not wanting to cancel any of those ministry opportunities.
Usually there are many victories for Jesus at these places. With the
doctor appointments scheduled for Thursday, January 3, the same
day that I was to be in Dallas, I was forced to cancel everything but
New Year's Eve and helping my son. While on the way to Denver on
Monday, I called the doctor to find out which medication I was to stop
taking. She had told me that one of them could interact with the dye
that would be injected into my blood, possibly causing liver damage.
Understanding that a working liver is essential for life, I thought it
would be worthwhile to call, while there was still about forty-eight
hours to be prepared. What I found out was that there had been a
mistake in scheduling, and even though I could see the doctor that
day, they would not be able to do the neck scan (sounds better than
a CAT scan), so there was no reason not to complete the remainder
of the planned mission trip, providing that the times were still open.
The medical appointments were all made for January 8, which was a
day when nothing had been previously scheduled.

The deceiver, my enemy the devil, had me imagining the worst that
could happen. Even though I had not done some of those things in over
thirty-five years that can cause cancer, the question remained: Were
my sins about to do me in or cause me to lose my voice? It would be
very difficult, if not impossible, to preach just using flash cards with
big, bold print, while standing silently, trying to add to the message
with expression and gestures. By not knowing sign language, except
for a few universally lewd gestures, and attempting to communicate
with people who would share my limitations, the usefulness of this
ministry would be greatly limited, but I didn't believe I would just
give up.

Because of the appointment date being changed, I called all the missions with whom I had canceled in hopes of still being able to share the love of Jesus to all of those dear folks, and praise the Lord, all were still open. I was delighted and praising the Lord, because if the worst did happen, and I would not be able to speak after seeing the doctors, at least I still would be able to lift my voice, telling many people of their urgent need to accept the gift of everlasting life in Jesus. On those three days, I witnessed thirty-six people decide that they wanted this relationship with Jesus, asking Him to be their Savior and Lord.

The big day came. Whatever would be would be. I was in the will of the Lord, and also trusting fully in His capable hands. I would do whatever I could to advance the gospel of Jesus Christ with whatever I would have left to work with. Everything went well except that the blood test and scan required hours of fasting (even one hour seems like a long time when hungry), and they were running a couple of hours late. After the scan, I was released to the cafeteria, where I could swallow again, and with gusto, I did just that.

It was finally time to see the specialist to learn the verdict of all the testing. While waiting in one of the rooms with posters of ear, nose, and throat parts, and an abundance of intriguing tools and machines to look at, and appreciating not seeing any sharp objects, one tool really caught my attention. It looked like an average-size flashlight with a display screen in place of lines, and a wire about the size and length of a long piece of overcooked spaghetti with a tiny camera on the end of it. A few weeks before, I had noticed a tool at a big hardware store that looked just like it, except it was a little larger, and written on the box was the description of what the tool was for. It was made to check for obstructions and other problems in drains and other hard-to-see places. Why would the doctor have something like that? It didn't take very long to find out. The doctor came in, looked down my throat, and pressed on my tonsils and neck. He then took the drain inspection tool and put the wire end into my left nostril. He gently went on a cave exploration trip, stopping along the way, perhaps to see the stalactites and stalagmites, and eventually inspecting the inner workings of my voice box. He had me make a few noises from low pitch to high, and when he had seen enough, he removed the tool.

He then told me that indeed I had an enlarged tonsil on the left side, but he did not know why. There was no cancer or anything else wrong that he could find. None of the tests showed any sign of even a potential problem.

Upon thanking him for his opinion, I told him that I was thankful to God for doctors. They are a gift to man, and are very valuable in helping us be healthy and alive; however, there is a Doctor that is greater than all others, and that is Jesus. Because of the swollen tonsil, there is evidence that there has been a problem, but I believe that the Great Physician, Jesus, had beaten him to it, and has already healed it. The doctor seemed to be in complete agreement.

This experience has once again shown me the importance of believing God's holy Word, the Bible, which states: *Trust in the LORD with all thine heart; and lean not unto thine own understanding. In all thy ways acknowledge him, and he shall direct thy paths* (Proverbs 3:5–6), as well as: *Come unto me, all ye that labour and are heavy laden, and I will give you rest. Take my yoke upon you, and learn of me; for I am meek and lowly in heart: and ye shall find rest unto your souls. For my yoke is easy, and my burden is light* (Matthew 11:28–30), and: *And Jesus, walking by the sea of Galilee, saw two brethren, Simon called Peter, and Andrew his brother, casting a net into the sea: for they were fishers. And he saith unto them, Follow me, and I will make you fishers of men* (Matthew 4:18–19).

In Conclusion: Jesus still wants people to believe in Him, and trust Him with their lives, as well as follow Him, telling others of His love for them. That is what I committed myself to do many years ago, after accepting Him as my Lord and Savior, and I have not changed my mind, nor have I ever regretted that decision. The yoke spoken of is the yoke that an ox would wear to pull a cart, and the matter of it being easy simply means that it would fit well, so that it would not hurt the ox as it labored in pulling a load with it. The light burden means that it will be something that God has prepared the bearer of the yoke to easily do, if he puts his will and actions into it. I find this all to be refreshingly true. My purpose in sharing this all with you is to encourage you to also follow Jesus, so that you too can realize the joy, peace, and satisfaction that He has for you.

CHAPTER 41

Religious Bondage

After having spoken of the loving mercy, grace, and salvation that Jesus chose to offer to all fallen people by giving His innocent life and blood for sinners like me, a man in his late sixties came to me asking if I could pray that he would be freed from the "bondage and superstitions" (his own words) of the religion that he had been born into and had remained in until now.

The religion of his parents was nothing that he had chosen and was not meeting his spiritual needs, so he wanted to be free from it but did not know how to attain that freedom. In all probability this was because he had been taught that he did not have direct access to God, but had to go through another person who could talk to Jesus' mother on his behalf, and, considering the nature of his request, this was not likely to happen. He must have suspected that I had the authority and connection to petition for his freedom to make his own choices concerning his beliefs. Again, the religion that he was trapped in was not meeting his spiritual needs or satisfying his soul. It had left him void of the peace, joy, and satisfaction that he longed for.

His situation was certainly not unique to any particular false religion, or the lack of religion, in that man was designed by God with the need to have an intimate relationship with his Creator. The problem was that most of us look for satisfaction and fulfillment of this natural longing in all the wrong places. Oftentimes people will look to some self-proclaimed religious guru, leader, or psychobabbler shrink who supposedly has the answers to life's questions, but they are people who are just as lost as the people they are trying to help, so the seekers are left with more questions than answers. Other people may try drugs, alcohol, illicit or inconvenient sexual encounters, or other sinful diversions in their quest for personal satisfaction. Yet others may try to lose themselves in games or other big-boy toys, such as cars, boats, sports, gambling, or other costly and time-consuming pastimes, that leave them empty and longing for satisfaction. Solomon tells us that all is vanity and vexation of our spirit.

The service was over and people had been invited to make decisions regarding their personal relationship with Christ. Many people out of the two hundred-plus had accepted Jesus as their hope of salvation and heaven, or had recommitted their lives to Him. This mission keeps a record of the decisions people make, so they can follow up by encouraging these people to learn about and live those commitments that they have just made. Another reason is so the mission can evaluate the effectiveness of their programs and that of the various speakers.

I was standing next to the pulpit gathering the completed decision cards, when this man brought me the card he had just filled out. He told me that he had done this several times before but felt he had not broken free of the traditions and superstitions of those things that he had been taught. He was hearing speakers actually take the Holy Bible and read, as well as explain, that having a personal relationship with Jesus was as simple as believing that Jesus is God's only Son by birth, and that He willingly died for fallen men, and was lifted from the dead by His Father God. If he only confessed that belief with his own mouth, he would be saved – saved from eternal damnation into everlasting life. But he said that he still felt trapped.

The prayer request that he presented to me was most unusual. I had never been asked this before, so to help this man receive peace of mind as well as eternal salvation, and believing that the living God does hear and answer the prayers of His children, I had to proceed. Right there in this crowded, noisy room, I told the man that I would lead him in a prayer that was not any secret formula or magic words, but it was what the Lord wants to hear from his heart. I would say the words and he could repeat after me, as though the words were coming from his heart and mind. This was simply talking to God with our own words, and telling Him what was on our heart and mind. These were not the exact words that we prayed, but they went something like this: "Dear God, we come to You in the name of Jesus, asking for Your help. I need to understand that You hear my prayers. I ask You to help me be free from the bondage of all superstitions and manmade rules, and in faith, I trust only in Your Word as stated in the Bible. I truly believe that Jesus gave His life as payment for my sins, so that by my free choice I can have life eternal with Him in heaven. I also ask You to be Lord of my life, admitting that You being Lord means that I give You control and authority in my life. Lord, give me courage to live for You, no matter what I used to do, or what others are doing around me. Lord, give me the courage to tell others of Your love for them. Thank You, Lord."

At the end of this prayer of faith I looked up, and he still had his head bowed and remained that way for a little while. I was beginning to wonder what was going on with him, but finally he looked up. He had a huge smile on his face, tears in his eyes, and he began telling me of the happiness and peace that had come over him, as well as the feeling of freedom. He said that he had never felt that way in his life. This was the end of our conversation for that day, but I did see him the next day.

Another service had ended, and several people were waiting to speak with me and have me pray with them regarding various matters. I noticed that the man who had been looking for spiritual freedom the day before was also waiting in line. When it was his turn, he told me that he had been telling others about Jesus, but he was scaring them so they didn't want to talk to him. He asked that I pray for him so he would not frighten others. If I thought that his first prayer request was unusual, this one was almost beyond belief, but he had asked me in innocent faith, so I had to respond, as I was silently praying, *Lord, give me the words to say that will help this man to be calm, wise as a serpent, but harmless as a dove. Let him continue in the joy of the Lord without causing others to be afraid of him.*

We prayed together again, and I do not remember exactly what was said, but whatever it was had a calming effect on the both of us, so we both went merrily on our way. I did see him again that day, and he seemed to be having a good day.

The reason this story is so special to me is that it is a reflection of my own personal history. I tell many people that I am from a crack drug family. Every time the door of the church was cracked, I was drug through it. Perhaps some of my children, relatives, or friends have felt that same way. I couldn't wait until I was free from that bondage, but that freedom brought even greater anxieties.

Finally a friend taught me that true freedom came from having a loving relationship with Jesus, by admitting that He (Jesus) loves me so much that He paid for my wrongdoings with His own blood. All He wants from me is to admit my need for Him. Upon my doing that, I felt as this other man did. Then I wanted to live a life pleasing to and for Jesus. I want to tell everyone I can of the freedom and joy I have found in Jesus.

Jesus loves YOU, dear Reader, just as much as He loves me or the other man. If you haven't already, won't you trust Jesus as your Lord and Savior now? Just admit to Jesus that you are a sinner, and you believe that He died for your sins and rose from the dead. He promises us that if we call on Him, He will save us for all eternity.

About the Author

I was born into a family of God-fearing people who did not rest in eternal security, always wondering if they would be good enough to go to heaven, or at least that is what I thought.

Because of my sinfulness, I figured I would not make it to heaven, so I lived like a lost person and became quite good at it, complete with bad habits and a foul mouth.

Sometime after seeing a dead man lying on a highway, hanging partway out of a truck windshield that was upside down on top of him, I began to wonder what would happen to me if I were that guy.

After some thought and reasoning, I realized that I had no hope of heaven, and would no doubt spend eternity in hell. That scared me very much, and I did not know what to do.

A Christian acquaintance saw me in that condition, noticed something really was bothering me, and asked what it was, so I told her. She told me how to have everlasting peace with God by asking Jesus to forgive me and save me. It would only require me to give my life to Him and follow Him.

At that point, I realized my life, as it was, was not worth living anyway, so I had nothing to lose. Even though I had asked Jesus to forgive me and take me to heaven when I died, I had never committed my life to following Him. That day I did accept Jesus as my Savior and guide, and things have never been the same since.

Jesus has given me peace where there was fear, joy in place of sorrow, a purpose in life other than self-service, and something worth doing. All that is left for me to say is, Thank you Jesus; I love you.

History of Sparrow Ministry

While on the pastoral staff at Blue Ridge Baptist Temple in 1986, I began speaking several times each month at City Union Mission in Kansas City, Missouri, and have spoken there on the third Tuesday of each month ever since.

In 2004, upon encouragement from the evening chaplain at City Union Mission, I began looking for other rescue missions to speak at, contacted several, got on their schedules, and began seeing good results. It became such a passion for me that I continued to get more involved.

The ministry began to grow to the point that we needed to form a not-for-profit organization, and we named it *Sparrow Ministry*, a ministry of North Grand River Baptist Association.

The name comes from a prior vocational occupation of mine of building birdhouses for the wholesale market, and realizing that no one ever asks for a sparrow house because no one seems to want sparrows around. They do not sing pretty and are very messy. That reminds me of the people we minister to, but thinking further, I realized that but for the grace and merciful forgiveness of God, I am just like them Because of that, I named it *Sparrow Ministry* instead of *Sparrows Ministry and I am that sparrow. I would never want any to think that I was talking down to the homeless.* In addition to that, I like what the Bible says about God and sparrows: *Are not two sparrows sold for a farthing? and one of them shall not fall to the ground without your Father* (Matthew 10:29).

We continue to go further, and speak more, and plan to keep expanding this ministry. It is the most exciting and rewarding adventure that I have been on in my life, and cannot imagine ever stopping, as long as the Lord allows.

Connect with Earl:

earlnance@sbcglobal.net

573-301-9736

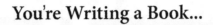